Desrene L. Vernon

Adventist World Radio Is On The Air: A Case Study Of Tanzania

Desrene L. Vernon

Adventist World Radio Is On The Air: A Case Study Of Tanzania

The Reactions of Local Listeners to International Religious Broadcasts

LAP LAMBERT Academic Publishing

Imprint

Any brand names and product names mentioned in this book are subject to trademark, brand or patent protection and are trademarks or registered trademarks of their respective holders. The use of brand names, product names, common names, trade names, product descriptions etc. even without a particular marking in this work is in no way to be construed to mean that such names may be regarded as unrestricted in respect of trademark and brand protection legislation and could thus be used by anyone.

Cover image: www.ingimage.com

Publisher:
LAP LAMBERT Academic Publishing
is a trademark of
International Book Market Service Ltd., member of OmniScriptum Publishing Group
17 Meldrum Street, Beau Bassin 71504, Mauritius

ISBN: 978-3-659-21821-7

Zugl. / Approved by: Washington DC, Howard University, Diss., 2011

DEDICATION

This book is dedicated to those who listen to and work with international religious radio broadcasts such as that of Adventist World Radio: Keep listening, keep working, "for in just a little while, He that shall come will come, and will not tarry" (Hebrews 10:37).

ACKNOWLEDGEMENTS

My deepest gratitude is extended to my mentors for providing guidance and support throughout the course of this study. Special thanks to Dr. Carolyn M. Byerly who both taught and modeled how to engage in mass communication and media scholarship. Special thanks to Dr. Barbara B. Hines for exemplifying leadership and always going the extra mile to find solutions. Thank you to Dr. Melbourne S. Cummings, for sharing her insights on how to examine ideologies critically and for helping me to appreciate the richness of rhetorical studies. Thank you to Dr. Sulayman S. Nyang, for exposing me to a wide range of African intellectuals, and for providing the context in which to examine religion and social change in Africa.

I would also like to thank Dr. Rhonda Zaharna of the School of Communication at American University for serving as my external examiner and for reminding us that technology should not replace interpersonal contacts. I hereby acknowledge Mwalimu Mkamburi Lyabaya, for sharing her expertise in Bantu languages and Swahili culture; Dr. Anita Nahal for being willing and available to share her insights on history and international affairs, and also Ms. Regina Drake for being a very gracious and supportive work supervisor.

This work would not be possible without the kindness and cooperation of Dr. Benjamin D. Schoun, and the Office of Archive and Statistics at the General Conference of Seventh-day Adventists. Thank you for being so open and accommodating from start to finish. Special thanks are also extended to Dr. Gaspar Colon, Mrs. Jane Ogora, and other members of the learning community of Washington Adventist University. Thank you Dr. Delyse Steyn of Andrews University, your mentorship and expertise are valued and greatly appreciated.

Table of Contents

LIST OF TABLES

LIST OF FIGURES

LIST OF ABBREVIATIONS

1. ABC: Adventist Book Center
2. ADRA: Adventist Development and Relief Agency
3. AIC: African Independent Churches
4. AID: Africa-Indian Ocean Division
5. ANN: Adventist News Network
6. AWR: Adventist World Radio
7. DOI: Diffusion Of Innovations
8. DRC: Democratic Republic of Congo
9. EAD: Eastern Africa Division
10. ECD: East-Central Africa Division
11. ELWA: Eternal Love Winning Africa (Liberia, West Africa, religious station)
12. ETC: East Tanzania Conference
13. FLF: Freedom Limitation Factor
14. GC: General Conference of Seventh-day Adventists
15. GDP: Gross Domestic Product
16. GMCF: Global Mission Challenge Factor
17. HCJB: Heralding Christ Jesus Broadcasting (Quito, Ecuador, religious station)
18. HIPC: Highly Indebted Poor Country
19. ICGC: International Central Gospel Church (Accra, Ghana)
20. IHFA: International Health Food Association
21. IMF: International Monetary Fund
22. IRB: International Religious Broadcasting
23. KBC: Kenyan Broadcasting Corporation

24.KDKA:	First Westinghouse radio station (Pittsburg, Pennsylvania)
25.MBS:	Madagascar Broadcasting System
26.MC:	Mara Conference
27.NETC:	North East Tanzania Conference
28.PCI:	Population Communication International
29.PSRC:	Parastatal Sector Reform Commission
30.RDB:	Radio Don Bosco (Madagascar, religious station)
31.RTLM:	Radio-Television Libre des Milles Collines
32.SDA:	Seventh-day Adventist
33.SHC:	South Highlands Conference
34.SNC:	South Nyanza Conference
35.TANU:	Tanganyika African National Union
36.TUM:	Tanzania Union Mission
37.UNFPA:	United Nations Population Fund
38.WTF:	West Tanzania Field
39.ZBC:	Zimbabwe Broadcasting Corporation

CHAPTER 1: INTRODUCTION

This is a case study examining the work of Adventist World Radio (AWR) in Tanzania, East-Central Africa. The study utilized a historical systematic methodology, to analyze archival documents relevant to AWR's operations. The goal was to determine the extent of a cause and effect relationship between the Seventh-day Adventist (SDA) church's media usage in east-central Africa, and the growth of the SDA church in Tanzania. The time period analyzed was 25 years, from 1983-2008. During this time frame the membership of the SDA church in the East-Central Africa Division (ECD) increased from 541 thousand members to nearly 2.1 million members, becoming the second largest membership division of the SDA church (Yost, 1983; Jones & Proctor, 2008). The church membership within the Tanzanian Union Mission (TUM) increased from 55 thousand in 1983 to nearly 308 thousand in 2003. By 2008, the membership within the TUM was more than 406 thousand.

The two and a half decades under investigation, were the same years in which the SDA church expanded its use of radio in the Africa region, beginning with AWR's first broadcast in French on Gabon's *Africa No.1* station in 1983; in English in 1987; to an expansive coverage of the African continent today with broadcasts in more than a dozen colonial and native languages including Kiswahili and Maasai, on both shortwave and local FM stations (AWR, 1981, 1988, 1994b). Given the comparative expansion of AWR's broadcast languages within the region, the creation of a programming studio in Morogoro, Tanzania, and the simultaneous membership growth in the SDA church in East-Central Africa, this study investigated whether there is a cause-effect relationship between the SDA church's use of radio, and the increase in the church's membership within the

TUM in East-Central Africa. To place the Tanzania Union Mission within the proper context, the SDA church's organizational structure will now be examined.

Organizational Structure of the SDA Church

The SDA church is a worldwide church with approximately 16 million members in more than 200 countries of the world (Jones & Proctor, 2009). The world is divided into 13 divisions with each geographic region forming a part of the worldwide structure which is administrated by the General Conference of Seventh-day Adventists (GC). The GC was officially organized in 1863 in Battle Creek, MI, USA. In 1903 the church's headquarters moved to Maryland, USA. The GC oversees operations of entities affiliated with the denomination, such as educational institutions, media outlets, medical facilities and publishing houses. The GC conducts its work worldwide through units called divisions which are expected to operate under the provisions of the organization's constitution, bylaws, and working policy (SDA Yearbook, 2011).

Of the 13 world divisions, four currently serve the continent of Africa. The first African division to be established was the Eastern Africa Division (EAD) which was formulated in 1970 to serve the countries of Djibouti, Eritrea, Ethiopia, Kenya, Somalia, Tanzania and Uganda. Through the years, as the SDA Church expanded, there have been several reorganization and restructuring initiatives which resulted in 2003 in the EAD merging with a portion of the African-Indian Ocean Division (AID) to create the East-Central Africa Division (ECD) of which Tanzania is a part. The other three African divisions are the Euro-Africa Division which serves Europe and North Africa, the Southern Africa-Indian Ocean Division which serves the countries of Southern Africa and the islands of the Indian Ocean, and the West-Central Africa Division (SDA Yearbook, 2010).

2

Within each world division is a managerial system consisting of unions, missions, conferences, mission fields, churches and companies, depending on the number of SDA members within the local population, and their ability to sustain their local organization financially. Within the TUM are five conferences, one field, more than three thousand churches and companies, and approximately 452 thousand members (Jones & Proctor, 2009). The organizational structure of the SDA Church, from the General Conference in Silver Spring, MD, to a local SDA member or AWR listener in Tanzania, can be diagrammed as depicted in Figure 1. Thus the SDA Church is organized, not as a series of separate national or regional churches, but as one worldwide, unified international church.

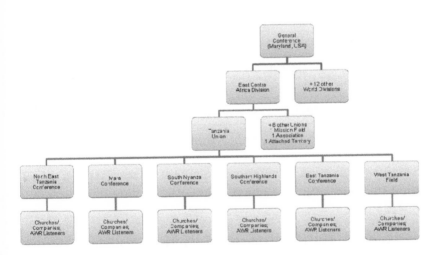

Figure 1: Organizational Structure of the SDA Church

According to the Adventist church's mission statement, its purpose is to proclaim the gospel to all peoples, leading them to accept Jesus and to unite with His church, in preparation for His return (SDA Yearbook, 2011). In keeping with this mission, the SDA Church engages in preaching, teaching, and healing, within an extensive network of institutions, corporations, services, and other entities. One such corporation is AWR which began in 1971 with a radio broadcast in Lisbon, Portugal. Since then AWR has expanded to create regional networks, namely: AWR-Europe (1971), AWR-America (1979), AWR-Africa (1983), AWR-Asia (1985), and AWR-Russia (1992). The following is a brief overview of AWR and AWR-Africa in particular as it is the network most central to this study.

Former AWR President, Ben Schoun, stated in *Transmissions* (2005, Autumn), that AWR's focus is on broadcasting the Adventist hope in Christ to the hardest-to-reach people groups of the world in their own languages. But behind the activities that move the network toward that mission, there is a necessary structure, which gives it organization, the ability to plan, and a means of being accountable. AWR's governing constituency is the executive committee of the GC. As stated earlier, AWR began in 1971, and the AWR-Africa network was formed in 1983. The purpose for these networks will now be examined.

Historical Development of Adventist World Radio

Adventist World Radio is the mission arm of the Seventh-day Adventist church, and it utilizes shortwave radio, FM, AM, Satellite and Internet broadcasting to spread its message (Backmer, 2007). It is devoted to international broadcasting of the gospel, particularly where conventional outreach methods, such as missionaries on the ground, are not available. When AWR began its ministry in

4

1971, it was specifically to preach the gospel to the people of the Soviet Bloc. According to Scragg and Steele (1996), the broadcasts were so effective that at times the government jammed the airwaves. The first program called *Adventist World Radio: the Voice of Hope* was aired on October 1, 1971, from the Radio Trans-Europe facility at Sines, Portugal. It was a small beginning: 10 hours per week in 12 languages. During the first six months on the air, the program received one thousand letters (Steele, 1996). Based on listener responses, church leaders began to see more and more the value of radio, especially in reaching otherwise unreachable areas. So as new opportunities for leasing time or building stations arose, the network expanded. As its name states, AWR has a global focus (AWR, 1985, 1988, 1991, 1993, 1994b, 1995b).

In 1979, AWR had its first broadcast in Latin America from Guatemala. Four years later, in October 1983, AWR started broadcasting in West Africa via a leased facility in Gabon. In 1985 AWR-Europe established a new short-wave facility in Italy, and after several more years of expansion, AWR-Russia was created in 1992 (AWR, 1999, 2001). By 1996, AWR had 18 transmitters at nine locations around the world, with broadcasts being aired in 33 languages (Scragg & Steele, 1996). Since then AWR has helped to launch several local FM stations thus scaling back its shortwave operations to three active networks: AWR-Africa; AWR-Asia, and AWR-Europe. Programs are now being produced in more than 80 languages with AWR-Africa broadcasting in more than 10 languages in east central Africa. AWR-Africa is responsible for broadcasts on the continent of Africa south of the Sahara, while AWR-Europe covers the countries of North Africa (AWR, 2001, 2007).

The preparation of interesting, uplifting and relevant programs directed to non-Christian listeners is the goal of AWR. Producers are chosen from the same language and cultural group as the target audience to increase the level of

5

connectivity with the people. A variety of program formats are used, with a magazine format being the most common. Segments can include short sermons, interviews, family matters, health information, drama, music, and programming for children. AWR does not have ratings information for their broadcasts. They acknowledge however, that general information on listening habits in select countries is available from one or two research organizations. To better serve the needs of their listening audiences, AWR has created regional networks. The remainder of this study will focus on one regional network, namely AWR-Africa.

AWR-Africa

Programs from AWR-Africa were first aired on *Africa No.1,* a leased facility in Gabon, West-Central Africa. The programs were divided into three main sections in which topics related to the Bible, education, and health were presented. According to a 1986 report from the Africa-Indian Ocean Division, there was a great demand for a health correspondence course and the division office strongly advised that one be made available to listeners (GC: AWR, 2001a-c). The 1986 Africa-Indian Ocean report also stated that in Benin, at least one baptism could be traced directly to the radio program. The local church had partnered with the radio network by sending a representative to deliver the correspondence course that was requested. Eventually the listener was baptized and began to serve as a secretary in the local church. A similar follow-up technique was documented in Senegal, which resulted in over 20 baptisms (AWR, 1985, 1993, 1994). The 1986 report proposed that the correspondence schools should be improved and local churches as well as their regional offices should be involved in the process of communicating with radio listeners. The writer of the 1986 Africa-Indian Ocean Division report noted: "as soon as possible we have to create strong ties between our listeners, churches, missions, and unions, in order to encourage people in this work where the results are most of the time hidden" (GC Adventist World Radio, 2001a).

Problem Investigated

The partnership between religion and the media extends back to the historical origins of the printing press, with the Bible being the first book to be mass produced. Likewise, in the early days of radio, a church service at the Pittsburgh Calvary Episcopal Church became the first live radio broadcast in 1921 (Christian History Institute, 2007). The partnership established between religion and the media many years ago continues today and remains vital to the expansion efforts of various religious organizations including the SDA church. AWR, established as the missionary arm of the SDA church, has an extensive worldwide network which would require multiple studies to analyze all of them. Consequently one regional network, AWR-Africa, has been chosen for this study.

This study sets forth a linkage between the religious broadcasts of AWR-Africa and the growth of the SDA church in Tanzania. Despite AWR-Africa's operations since 1983, no study appears to have been conducted to measure the contributions it has made to the growth of the SDA church. To date, the East-Central Africa Division is the second largest of the 13 world divisions, and accounts for a significant percentage of the population of the world church. The Tanzania Union Mission, along with several other African Unions, have been experiencing rapid church growth which necessitates frequent reorganization of the divisions in an attempt to provide appropriate leadership and support for the work of the church at various levels. Yet, no study has been conducted to determine the contributions made by religious radio broadcasts.

7

Research Question (RQ)

One overarching research question was selected for this study along with five more specific subcomponents.

RQ 1: *To what extent has Adventist World Radio succeeded in fulfilling the Seventh-day Adventist Church's mission in Tanzania?*

The church's mission is based on the verses of scripture outlined in the gospel of Matthew: 28:18-20[1] and placed in the context of the three angels' messages of Revelation 14: 6-12. The church's mission statement can be divided into four parts: (1) proclaiming the Christian message to all nations, kindred, tongue and people, (2) leading them to accept Jesus and (3) uniting with His church, while (4) nurturing them in preparation for His soon return (SDA Yearbook, 2011). In an effort to carry out this mission, there is an AWR studio located in Morogoro, Tanzania, which produces the Kiswahili and Maasai language broadcasts. This study investigated the overarching question by examining the following more specific research questions:

RQ 1a: What factors contribute to the SDA church's engagement in the use of religious radio broadcasts to fulfill their stated global mission within the Tanzania Union Mission?

RQ 1b: How has AWR's expansion of broadcast languages to include Maasai language programs, contributed to the growing number of Adventist members within the Tanzania Union Mission?

RQ 1c: Which AWR programs have listeners indicated a preference for by specifically identifying them in their correspondences?

---

[1] "And Jesus came and spoke to them, saying, "All authority has been given to Me in heaven and on earth. Go therefore and make disciples of all the nations, baptizing them in the name of the Father and of the Son and of the Holy Spirit, teaching them to observe all things that I have commanded you; and lo, I am with you always, even to the end of the age." Amen" (The Bible: New King James Version).

8

RQ 1d: What reasons did AWR listeners in Tanzania express for corresponding with the AWR network?

RQ 1e: In what ways have AWR listeners within Tanzania, conveyed to the network an interest in learning more about Adventism?

These research questions were answered by analyzing archival documents available from the AWR network as well as the SDA Office of Archives and Statistics. Sources included personal communications, studio reports, listener correspondences, promotional DVDs and organizational documents. The study focused on the first 25 years of AWR-Africa's existence, from 1983-2008, which also intersected with the centennial celebration of the SDA church's presence in Tanzania from 1903 to 2003. To better understand the overlapping disciplines of this study, several key terms are defined alphabetically.

Terms Central to the Study

Baptism (Gr. *Baptisma,* from *baptizō* "to dip," "to immerse")

According to the *SDA Encyclopedia* (Neufeld, 1996), baptism is a Christian initiation ritual which can be performed by immersion, pouring, or sprinkling. The SDA Church believes in "baptism by immersion," and sees the process as typifying the death, burial, and resurrection of Jesus Christ. A baptismal candidate is expected to openly express faith in God's saving grace and the repudiation of sin and the world. Baptism is recognized as a condition of entrance into SDA church membership (*SDA Church Manual,* 1990, as cited in Neufeld, 1996).

Baptisms are usually conducted by ordained ministers but if none are available, a local church elder could officiate with the approval of the conference president (*Manual for Ministers,* 1992 as cited in Neufeld, 1996). Persons entering

9

the SDA Church who have been baptized by immersion in other religious communities are accepted on profession of faith, without baptism, unless they desire to be re-baptized.

Church Membership

Admission into SDA church membership is usually granted after three prerequisites are met. The first is conversion, followed by an acceptance of the principles and doctrines of the SDA Church, and thirdly, baptism by immersion. Those complying with these prerequisites are granted membership by vote of the local members. For those requesting admission by baptism, the vote may be taken prior to baptism (that is "subject to baptism") or after baptism. Members usually welcome the newly baptized by extending to them "the right hand of fellowship."

Evangelicalism

According to the *Encyclopedia of Religion* (Eliade, 1987), the term *evangelicalism* usually refers to the following: (1) a largely Protestant movement that emphasizes the Bible as authoritative and reliable; (2) eternal salvation as possible only by regeneration (being "born again"), which involves personal trust in Christ and in His atoning work; (3) a spiritually transformed life marked by moral conduct, personal devotion such as Bible reading and prayer; and (4) a zeal for evangelism and missions.

Evangelical designates a distinct movement that emerged from the religious awakenings of the eighteenth century in America, England, the British Empire, and many of their mission fields.

Evangelism, Public

Seventh-day Adventists believe that evangelism--the proclamation of the gospel--is the very heart of Christianity. From the early days of the SDA Church, public evangelism has played a major role in the growth and development of the denomination. One of the church's founders, Ellen G. White encouraged evangelism efforts by her periodical articles, special testimonies, personal counsels and addresses over the years; many of her writings have been collected and published as a book titled *Evangelism*.

As times changed, methods have also changed, and evangelism has come to include radio and television programs, correspondence lessons, and Revelation and Prophecy seminars, among other programs. International programs produced by broadcasting entities such as the *Voice of Prophecy, Faith for Today, Breath of Life*, and *It Is Written* are a focal point for evangelism. Since 1972 a yearly coordinated evangelistic thrust has been adopted in many world divisions. These have been designated as *MISSION '72, '73, '74, '75; Thousand Days of Reaping, Harvest 90,* and *Global Mission. MISSION '75* inaugurated an integrated health evangelism approach known as the *Century 21 Better Living Institute.*

International Religious Broadcasting (IRB)

International Religious Broadcasting is the term favored by sociologists; media studies scholars, and students of international broadcasting. Some argue that it is the contemporary term for "missionary radio" which is used by historians and includes a chronological dimension, linked to a specific phenomenon, that of the modern Protestant missionary movement. These terms connote the specific religious meaning and missionary purpose that conservative Protestant groups in the United States attached to the use of radio overseas. Radio used for missionary purposes have also been termed "Mechanical Missionaries" (Stoneman, 2007). In

11

this study, the terms missionary radio and mechanical missionaries will be used interchangeably.

Missiology

Missiology is the scholarly study of the Christian mission. *Missiologists* are religious scholars engaged in the study of missions. Missiology as a discipline was not supported by a professional association until the formation of the Association of Professors of Missions in 1952 (Carpenter & Shenk, 1990). Skreslet (2007) recognizes that in the study of missiology, "complete objectivity is certainly beyond our grasp, but a measure of transparency regarding intentions and interests can be achieved" (Skreslet, 2007, p. 60). Skreslet goes on to state that it is only via these means that the historical work of scholars within the field, can hope to earn any degree of lasting respect from present and future generations (Skreslet, 2007).

Proselytism

The word *proselytism* is derived ultimately from the Greek language, and literally means stranger or foreign sojourner (Cross & Livingstone, 1997). Historically the word denoted a person who had converted to the Jewish religion, but today the word proselytism is also used to refer to other religions' attempts to convert people to specific religious beliefs, faith or sect; or even any attempt to convert people to another point of view, religious or not. In contemporary societies the connotations of the word proselytism are often negative but this study will use the word neutrally to refer to any attempts to convert a person or people to another faith.

A theological distinction is now made between "proselytism" and "witness." It started at the beginning of the 20th century, with Christian missionaries seeking ways to avoid competition among them. Religious tolerance was furthered by

12

Article 18 of the 1948 Universal Declaration on Human Rights, which recommended that freedom of thought, conscience and religion be incorporated into national legal systems. Words like proselytism, implying coercion, manipulation or deception, gave way to words such as dialogue and witness. The idea that faith and belief require free choice and should not be coerced also emerged (Pew Research Center, 2010, p. 6). For the purpose of this study, the terms will be used interchangeably.

Protestant

The term *Protestant* was first applied to Lutherans in 1529. The term was historically created in reference to German princes and free cities who formally protested to the Diet of Spires and its decision to uphold the edict of the Diet of Worms against the Reformation (Neufeldt, 1997). Now Protestants refer to any member of the various Christian churches not belonging to the Roman Catholic or Eastern Orthodox Church. The term has become so inclusive that it is difficult to provide a precise definition, but Cross and Livingstone (1997), offer the following guidelines in terms of what Protestants believe. Protestants accept the Bible as the sole source of revealed truth, the doctrine of justification by faith alone, and the universal priesthood of all believers. This last principle has led Protestants to reject any kind of two tier spirituality such as clerical or monastic, preferring to emphasize more lay person spirituality based upon personal Bible reading, and a high standard of personal morality. In general, Protestant worship has been marked by the participation of the whole congregation, by the public reading of the Bible and an emphasis on preaching.

13

The Seventh-day Adventist Church (SDA)

This Christian church began in North America, and has since expanded around the world. In 1860, the name Seventh-day Adventist was chosen for the denomination's identity. In 1942, their first radio broadcast (*The Voice of Prophecy*), was launched in the United States, and 30 years later, Adventist World Radio was created as an international religious broadcasting entity. The church's global membership is approximately 16 million (SDA Yearbook, 2011).

Union (Union Conference; Union Mission)

A unit of church organization formed by a group of several local conferences, missions or fields, which in turn form a constituent part of the GC in one of its geographical divisions. The union conference organization is similar to that of the local conference, and it is governed by a constitution and bylaws. In areas in which the church is not self-sustaining, the union organization (called a union mission or simply a union) appoints the officers of the local missions, fields, etc.

CHAPTER 2: RELIGION AND CULTURE IN EAST-CENTRAL AFRICA

Chapter two focuses on religion, politics, language and culture. The chapter begins with a summation of the Pew Research Center's *Forum on Religion & Public Life* which was conducted in sub-Saharan Africa in 2008-2009. This is followed by a more in depth look at religion, culture and politics as societal forces within Tanzania. The ground work laid by Christian missionaries will also be examined along with the natives' response to the new religious ideas being brought into the culture. The chapter concludes with a chronology of the development of Adventism in Tanzania from the arrival of the first SDA missionaries in 1903, to the SDA Church's present scope of operations.

Religion and Public Life in East-Central Africa

Tanzania was one of 19 countries involved in the Pew Research Center's study (2010). The Pew Research Center sought to analyze how sub-Saharan Africans viewed the role of religion in their lives and societies. A survey was administered in more than 60 languages, to respondents in each of the countries selected. In Tanzania, both English and Kiswahili were used among the 1,500 participants. Two thirds of the Tanzanian respondents were Christians, and one third was Muslim. The Tanzanian sample was nationally representative of the adult population and included participants from all regions including Zanzibar (Unguja and Pemba), and was proportional to the urban and rural segments of the population (Pew Research Center, 2010). Ninety-three percent of the respondents from Tanzania ranked religion as very important in their lives. This was the highest ranking among the east African countries involved in the study.

Another interesting finding of the Pew Forum was that both Christianity and Islam were flourishing in sub-Saharan Africa, which suggested that neither faith may expand as rapidly in the years ahead as it did in the 20th century, except possibly through natural population growth. One of the main reasons presented for this conclusion was that 90% of the people in the region were already fully committed to Christianity or Islam, which meant that the pool of potential converts from outside these two faiths was very small. In Tanzania, sixty percent of those surveyed identified themselves as Christian and 36% as Muslim, with only 2% identifying solely with traditional African religions, and 1% as unaffiliated (Pew Research Center, 2010).

The Pew Research Center also noted that there was little evidence based on their findings, to indicate that either Christianity or Islam was growing at the expense of the other. There was a small percentage of Muslims who had become Christians, and a relatively small percentage of Christians who had become Muslims, but the survey found no substantial shift in either direction. In Tanzania, 58% of the respondents were raised as Christians, with 60% of those surveyed identifying themselves as currently Christians. This resulted in a net change of only 2 %. Similarly, 35% of those surveyed indicated that they were raised Muslim, while 36% indicated that they were currently Muslim (Pew Research Center, 2010, p. 12).

Within Christianity, there was also no significant religious switching taking place among denominations. Thirty-two percent of the Tanzanian sample said they were raised Catholic, while 31% said they were currently Catholic. Twenty three percent said they were raised Protestant and 27% identified themselves at the time as Protestants (Pew Research Center, 2010, p. 24). The Pew Research Center also

16

found that Adventists had a greater percentage of followers in Zambia, but were only 3% in Tanzania, while Anglicans accounted for roughly 10% or more of the Christian respondents in Tanzania (Pew Research Center, 2010, p. 22). Religious commitment, as demonstrated by church attendance, was also very high in the region. The majority in every country surveyed said they attended religious services at least once per week, and in most countries more than three-in-four people reported attending worship services weekly or more. In Tanzania, 83% of the sample said they attended religious services regularly (Pew Research Center, 2010, p. 27).

Large majorities of Christians and Muslims in all the countries surveyed said they often read religious pamphlets, magazines, newspapers and books, and in most countries large numbers also said they listened to religious radio or watched religious television programs. In Tanzania, 55% of the sample indicated that they prayed at least once per day (Pew Research Center, 2010, p. 28). Substantial numbers of Christians and Muslims in all the countries surveyed saw it as their duty to convert others to their faith. The actions of both Muslims and Christians also indicated a strong desire to pass their religious values on to their children. The majority of Christian and Muslim parents in nearly all the countries surveyed said they prayed or read scriptures with their children, and also sent their children to religious education programs (Pew Research Center, 2010, p. 30).

Another finding of the Pew Research Center's study was that in every country with a substantial Christian population, at least half of the Christians expect that Jesus will return to earth during their lifetime. In Tanzania, this belief was held by 62 % of the survey participants (Pew Research Center, 2010, p. 13). Both Christians and Muslims believe they are living in a time that will undergo momentous religious events and they would be alive to witness them. Looking forward with hope seemed natural to survey respondents given that unemployment

17

was commonly cited as a major problem. Across the region, many people reported struggling to afford life's basic necessities. Religious leaders and movements therefore remain a major force in civil society and a key provider of relief and development for the needy, especially where government agencies are unable to do so.

Half or more of respondents in at least 12 of the countries surveyed said there had been times in the last year when they were unable to afford food, clothing or medical care. Tanzanian respondents scored the lowest in their level of optimism about the future, in comparison to the other 18 sub-Saharan countries (Pew Research Center, 2010, p. 56). Religion can therefore be viewed as a source of hope as various denominations strife to provide in the present, some of the basic physical necessities of life while offering spiritual guidance for life in the future.

East central Africa is among the most religious places in the world, yet many international religious organizations still consider the region a mission field. Other factors contributing to this designation include population figures, mortality and literacy rates, as well as health and economic challenges. The next segment examines the historical context of religion and development within the region, followed by a more in-depth profile of the country of Tanzania.

Religion and Development in East Central Africa

Religious missionaries in Africa were always part of more general cultural and economic flows. Islam moved with traders along the east coast, across North Africa and the Sahara, and down, inland, into the west. Christianity moved with the expansion of Europe, down the west coast and into the middle of sub-Saharan Africa. As a result, there is an area across the sub-Sahara where both religions are prevalent. There are many stories of Africans moving from one Christian faith to another in order to advance their education, obtain jobs or other essential services.

18

Both Islam and Christianity, albeit in different ways, have opened up the world to Africans, bringing in outsiders and also linking Africans to their respective networks and communication systems. Both groups assure their members that they are a part of a global community based on a belief in a single omnipotent God and a single human race where all are equal. To an oppressed minority, this is an especially appealing message (Pew Research Center, 2010). The Pew Forum noted that Tanzanians were among respondents who were the most pessimistic about the future. What are the socio-economic conditions prevalent in Tanzania that may have influenced this outlook?

Tanzania: Country Profile

The United Republic of Tanzania, formerly known as German East Africa, then Tanganyika, took its current name upon uniting with Zanzibar in 1964. It shares borders with the Democratic Republic of Congo (DRC) on the west, Burundi and Rwanda to the northwest, Uganda and Kenya to the north, and Mozambique, Malawi and Zambia towards the south. The Indian Ocean borders its eastern shore. Though it shares its borders with eight countries, it has managed to remain largely peaceful with its neighbors. Tanzania is the only east African nation that has two capital cities: Dar es Salaam is its commercial capital, and Dodoma, its administrative capital. The country's population is approximately 44 million (The World Bank, 2011), and is administrated in 26 regions including the islands of Mafia, Pemba and Zanzibar.

Ninety nine percent of the country's population consists of more than 120 African ethnic groups, the largest of which are the Sukuma and the Nyamwezi.

None of the ethnic groups however, exceed 10% of the population. The remaining one percent of the population is comprised of Arabs, Asians and Europeans (Berry, 2003). More than 69% of the population can read and write Kiswahili (Swahili), English, or Arabic. The life expectancy at birth is 56 years (The World Bank, 2011). The country is home to more than a half-million refugees (more than any other African country), mainly from Burundi and DRC, yet it has been spared the internal strife that has devastated many African states (CIA World Fact Book, 2010).

In 1954 the Tanganyika African National Union (TANU) was created, and seven years later the country became the first independent nation in east Africa. The first president, Julius Nyerere, called *Mwalimu* by the people (Swahili word for teacher; used as a title), introduced a socialist system of government and, urging national self-reliance, he resisted economic dependence on foreign countries. The government focused its attention on the alleviation of illiteracy, poverty and disease, and pursued a policy of nationalizing important economic sectors, particularly major industries, distribution and marketing. After years of economic hardships however the nation faced economic collapse in 1985 and Mwalimu Nyerere voluntarily left office (Van Buren, 2003). In order for the new government under President Ali Hassan Mwinyi, to receive international aid, a series of restructuring initiatives had to be put in place including the privatization of many industries. This led to the establishment of the Parastatal Sector Reform Commission (PSRC) to oversee the privatization process (Murison, 2003).

Agriculture remains the mainstay of Tanzania's economy, providing a livelihood for more than 80% of the population. The main food crop is maize, with coffee, cassava, paddy rice, sorghum, plantains, sweet potatoes, beans and millet produced in large quantities. Since 1999, cashew exceeded coffee as the country's main export crop. Tanzania is also one of Africa's largest cattle producers, with an

20

estimated national herd of 14.4 million heads in 2000 (Murison, 2003). Though Tanzania remains one of the poorest countries in the world, with more than one third of the population living below the poverty line, it has had some success with donors and investors.

According to Freedom House (2010), Tanzania has a world freedom index of 4 (on a scale of 1-7, with 1 being most free and 7 being least free) for political rights, and a score of 3 for civil liberties. The press is considered partly free, as the constitution provides for freedom of speech, but several laws limit the ability of the media to function effectively. The island of Zanzibar is more restrictive than the mainland as journalists are required to be licensed and must obtain a permit prior to covering police activities. The state also prohibits any independent radio or television broadcasts from the island although its residents can receive private broadcasts from the mainland. In 2009 internet penetration for the entire country was only one percent but there was an increasing trend with the opening of more internet cafes and service providers.

Tanzania has been ruled by both Christian and Muslim leaders in the past. While both religious viewpoints are distinctly different, the country remains unified, and has experienced rather peaceful political transitions. Let us examine a bit more closely the dynamics of religion and politics in Tanzania.

Religion and Politics in Tanzania

Christianity and Islam have coexisted in Tanzania for many years. Tanzania's first president was a Christian (Julius Nyerere), and he handed over power in 1985 to a Muslim leader (Ali Hassan Mwinyi). Ten years later, Mwinyi handed over to a Christian leader, Benjamin Mkapa. During these transitions, religion did not play a significant role even though there remained problems arising from the union between the mainland (with a fairly even balance between Christian and Muslim populations) and the island of Zanzibar (where the population is about 96 percent Muslim). Given Zanzibar's predominantly Muslim population, some Zanzibaris preferred to associate with the wider Islamic world rather than look towards the mainland of Tanzania (Forster, 1997). Forster believed however that religious diversity would remain in mainland Tanzania, and that it was unlikely that any serious proposals would arise that would change the secular state currently in existence there.

The first Tanzanian president, Mwalimu Nyerere, embraced the doctrine of *ujamaa* (socialism) which appealed to traditional African notions of sharing and family solidarity. Christian and Muslim teachings were both invoked in its support. But despite the appeal to tradition, indigenous religion was not invoked on an equal footing with Christianity and Islam as it was more likely to be seen as unprogressive (Forster, 1997). Nyerere was especially critical of Christians, far more so than he was of Muslims. He stressed the importance of economic development, and maintained that poverty stemmed from lack of social justice rather than from shortages (Forster, 1997).

Some religious denominations such as the Jehovah's Witnesses experienced a clear conflict with the state. They were officially condemned for lack of interest in development, and for apparent opposition to ujamaa. Some were arrested, though measures taken fell short of statutory prohibition, and in practice the sect continued to function. There were for similar reasons some short-term conflicts with Pentecostals and Seventh-day Adventists (Forster, 1997). According to Forster (1997), the problem was that of religion being much more concerned with the "next" world, paying only minimal attention to the here-and-now, which created difficulties for a country striving to build national identity and development.

22

In Nyerere's Tanzania, religious organizations were supported by the state on condition that their teachings conformed to values which the state endorsed. Muslims, Christians and followers of traditional religion all held some beliefs which could be hostile to national integration and to state ideology. Nyerere expected these to be toned down, with priority being given to aspects of the relevant religious tradition which could be presented as legitimizing state ideology (Forster, 1997). The state has remained supreme in secular matters, but in return it guarantees freedom of worship. Believers in a particular religion remain free to seek converts, but not in a way which insults other faiths. This policy has led to some supervision of religious meetings, including the need for permits, especially when preachers from outside Tanzania have been involved (Forster, 1997).

The government has also welcomed the education and health services provided by religious bodies. These not only reduce cost to the government, but also reflect the philosophy that religion is concerned with the body as well as the soul. Mwinyi returned hospitals and schools nationalized under the Nyerere government to their previous owners. In 1990 constitutional provision was made for freedom of religion, combined with recognition that conduct and management of religious communities was not part of the function of the state. Religious teaching has been seen by the government however as important for moral instruction, especially in the face of "foreign behavior." Islam and Christianity have been presented as sharing the same goals, with religion in schools having the capacity "to correct false impressions of other faiths" (Forster, 1997, p.171). Religious principles are also evident in the cultural life of Tanzania. The following review of Topan's (1973) literary work (as cited in Kruisheer, 1999) highlights the parody of religion, especially when its ideological tenets are not adhered to in daily living.

23

Language and Culture in Tanzania

Kruisheer (1999) conducted a literary criticism of the Zanzibarian playwright Farouk Topan's Swahili play, *Aliyeonja Pepo* (A Taste of Heaven). The play was published in 1973 and has been on the required reading list for secondary schools for many years. In describing the play, Kruisheer (1999) wrote:

The play is built on symbolic and implication techniques typical of the school that emerged during the post-independence period of Tanzania that took theater as a means of communication with the masses, producing works of public and historic interest and social impact. (p. 44)

Aliyeonja Pepo is set in Heaven, or as the author explains, "an image of Heaven inspired by East African Islamic beliefs" (Kruisheer, 1999, p. 44). Unfortunately, the events which transpire are less than ideal. One of the main characters, the angel of death Ziraili, is responsible to organize the transfer of human souls from Earth to Heaven, but due to his administration's incompetence, a soul is brought to Heaven too early and has to be sent back to Earth (Kruisheer, 1999, p. 44). The soul that is enjoying his untimely taste of heaven is a fisherman from Bagamoyo, called Juma Hamisi; the one left on Earth is an Englishman from Bournemouth by the name of John Houghton (Kruisheer, 1999, p. 47).

Juma Hamisi was enjoying his stay in Heaven until he was notified that he was there by accident. He vehemently opposed being returned to Earth-even more so when he hears that his soul would return in the body of an Englishman (Kruisheer, 1999). "The ideological demonization of 'the other' is so strong, that Hamisi would rather suffer dehumanization--become a cat—within his own

24

ideological world, than be converted into another human in the ideological world of the other" (Kruisheer, 1999, p. 54).

Kruisheer (1999) reports that he found only two references to the play throughout his study and both emphasized the religious content. One of the references was a review by P.S. Kirumbi which was published in the Tanzanian magazine on literatures, *Mulika* (1975). Kirumbi first praises the author [Farouk Topan] for his courage to create such a work, but, in the course of his review, he actually accuses him of *Kejeli* (ridicule, blasphemy). According to Kirumbi, by presenting a Heaven where mistakes are made, the play questions the existence of Heaven and the heavenly angels and calls into question the character of the almighty God. The second comment on Aliyeonja Pepo can be found in the standard work *Outline of Swahili Literature* by Bertoncini (as cited in Kruisheer, 1999). By presenting a lively summary, Bertoncini's report strongly emphasizes the "comic vein" of the play. Bertoncini believed that the play dealt with the role of religion in modern society and the question of how a religious man should behave on earth (Kruisheer, 1990).

Topan's foreword reveals great concern from his side about the position of religion in what he calls "modern times." It starts with a digression on the history of mankind; leading to the proposition that religion nowadays appears to function merely as a support to the other main systems society relies upon such as politics and education. It has lost its traditional role in the society as a whole and has become a mere individual affair, serving only those who are concerned about their fate after death. Accordingly, the author raises the following question at the end of his foreword: "[I]f religion has reached this stage; will then religion truly be religion?" (Kruisheer, 1999, p. 45).

Kruisheer (1999) "seeks to reconstruct what the author's intended message might have been" arguing that "the main act was most probably meant as a sociopolitical, rather than a religious, parody" (p. 46). Some of the religious images incorporated in the play, include "the concept of a place called Paradise, located in Heaven, where men have unlimited access to virginal, lovely girls," just as the character, Juma Hamisi, experienced. The play however, presents a Heaven that does not seem very heavenly; a messy office where administration is not carried out properly, where the workers take it easy, and the highest authority has to be informed of daily activities by means of a telephone connection. The angels, trusted to be pure and divine, are presented as lazy and phony creatures that make incredible mistakes. One of them, Ziraili, even enjoys alcoholic beverages in spite of the taboo. The angel who was supposed to have enough air to blow the horn at the end of time turns out to be addicted to cigars and was already coughing his lungs out. "The play owes much of its comic impact to this presentation of affairs" (Kruisheer 1999, p. 48).

At the time the play was published in 1973, the Republic of Tanzania was still within its first decade of existence. The TANU elected before the country's official date of Independence in 1961, set out to establish a socialist policy under the name of Ujamaa. Under the leadership of the founder of the Ujamaa ideology, Mwalimu Nyerere, an elaborate bureaucratic apparatus had been formed. It can be surmised that Topan's "angels" are meant to represent the fast growing body of civil servants who started working in the offices of Tanzania in the 1960s (Kruisheer, 1999, p. 48).

Ziraili explains in the first act that the angels in the play work according to a so-called *Mpango wa Miaka Saba* (Seven Year Plan). Every seven years *Bwamkubwa* (the angels' boss) plans which human souls should be taken from Earth in the coming seven years. Thus the author has molded the religious concept of predestination into a bureaucracy. The concept of these Seven Year Plans appears to be a copy of the Five Year Plans, which were created for the Republic of Tanzania by the political leaders (Kruisheer, 1999). In a third act dialogue between two characters in the play, Sirafili and Juma Hamisi, the fisherman (Hamisi) protests against being sent back to Earth. Sirafili is impressed by Juma's arguments only when he brings in *utamaduni wa kitaifa,* (national culture), actually using rhetoric of the Ujamaa ideology. The things the angels do that are so to speak, "improper for angels," are literally the same things that the citizens of the country of Ujamaa, that Tanzania was to become, were not supposed to do. In Nyerere's readings it is often emphasized that the country needed labor in the first place, and that: "laziness, drunkenness and idleness should be things to be ashamed of" (Kruisheer, 1999, p. 50).

Kruisheer (1999) concluded that the question remained as to what such a parody might reveal regarding the status of religion in the Tanzanian society of the 1960s. Kruisheer argued that:

If Bwamkubwa stands for Nyerere, this means that the former leader of Tanzania is thus represented at the level of God, which elevates his ideas to the same level as the religion of Islam. By linking Ujamaa ideology to the word *Imani* (belief/ faith/ creed), which is mostly used in a religious context, it is even suggested that the people should have faith in this ideology in the same way that they confess to their religious stand. By subsequently breaking several codes that are part of the religious concept, the ideology of Ujamaa is examined, or, as it was characterized above, parodied and one of its fundamental ideas thus ridiculed. (Kruisheer, 1999, p. 51)

As was explained in the reading, everything that is *kijamaa* (socialist) is presented as correct or "good," while anything that inclines to *kibepari* (capitalist), ways was presented as wrong, bad, or evil. Just as a religious man is urged to turn

27

to his religion and pray to God when confronted with evil, the readings implied that kibepari ways can be countered by holding on to the principles of Ujamaa. The parody in the main act appears to show the ridiculousness of the idea that a political ideology could be confessed like a religion, for this would not leave people much room for a religious life. Taken together with the Devil's epilogue and the question of good and evil, the message emerges that an answer to such questions cannot and does not have to be found by political leaders, as long as their ideologies allow space for religion too (Kruisheer, 1999).

While Kruisheer's discourse centered on a play in the form of a religious parody, it helped to reveal the integral role religion played in the fabric of Tanzanian society. The play mixed both Christian and Islamic imagery very well because both religions have much in common. Christianity and Islam come from related theological traditions, and both believe in a single omnipotent God who is concerned with human history and who has sent messengers to guide human beings from earth to heaven (Martin, 1998). According to Martin (1998) "both religions view the tolerance of other religions with difficulty; and both religions are Universalist, appealing to and welcoming all human beings" (p. 401). While both religions decry all forms of discrimination on grounds such as gender, nationality, and ethnic origin, each still has conservative and radical elements. In addition, Christianity and Islam have been transplanted to many different cultures and both remain committed to recruiting new members throughout the world. Overall, Christianity has placed a greater emphasis than Islam however on administrative structures as mechanisms of unity. This can now be seen in the following discourse on the development of Christian missions in Tanzania.

Christian Missions in Tanzania

In 1890, Great Britain and Germany agreed to establish the Songwe River as the boundary of their zones of influence in the region between Lake Nyasa and Lake Tanganyika. Consequently, the Nyakyusa became part of the newly established colony of German East Africa, which comprised, in addition to Tanganyika, Rwanda and Burundi (Wright, 1971, as cited in Gabbert 2001). German Protestant missionary societies soon replaced British missionaries already working in the area. The mission fields were delimited by mutual agreements. According to Gabbert (2001), the term Nyakyusa denotes the linguistically and culturally related chiefdoms located at the northern end of Lake Nyasa between the Songwe River and the Livingstone Mountains in the southwestern parts of Tanzania. Their economy is based on cattle herding and cultivation of food crops. It was the British colonial administration who decided to use the self-identification of certain chiefly lineages of the highlands (aba-nyakyusa) as a designation for the entire population of the area north of the Songwe River (Gabbert, 2001, p. 295).

Since missionaries possessed "magical skills," had items that the natives found attractive (such as gun powder and pain killers), and presented opportunities for wage labor, they were generally accepted by the local population (Gabbert, 2001, pp. 297-298). The acceptance of missionaries was also facilitated because Nyakyusa attitudes towards strangers were not necessarily negative. "Europeans were frequently categorized as chiefs bringing peace and cloth; however spreading the gospel, which the missionaries considered their real task, met with little interest." The presence of missionaries in the area also meant a certain amount of protection against abuse by the *Askaris* (African soldiers of the colonial administration) (Gabbert, 2001, p. 298).

Gabbert (2001) noted that social and economic transformations were accompanied by a rapid increase in the number of Christians. A mere 21 individuals converted to Christianity in 1898, while more than 2,000 Africans were baptized in 1914. By 1930 the number of Christians in Nyakyusa had risen to almost 10,000. Gabbert (2001) noted that:

> The establishment of a system of Western education played a decisive role in this growth process. Education of the "heathen" was an essential component of missionary work from the start, since Moravians and other Protestant churches stressed the importance of a thorough knowledge of the Bible by the faithful. The educational opportunities offered by the missionaries however, evoked very little enthusiasm at first. Parents frequently had to be convinced by small sums of money or presents of salt or cloth to send their children to school. Thus, going to school was considered a kind of wage labor for the missionaries. (p. 299)

Attitudes towards missionary education began to change in 1904, when it became obvious that under colonial rule an education was essential to being able to transact in a money economy. Africans began to realize the benefits of being literate and saw the difference it made in acquiring jobs such as "a mission helper, teacher, government clerk, tax collector, or employee on a European plantation" (Gabbert, 2001, p. 300). Christian schools were the only option in some regions hence both Christian and education were joined in the minds of many Africans for a long time.

Moravian missionaries fostered development by denying the power of "superstitious beliefs" thus weakening the authority of the lineage elders and made it easier for the young to abandon traditional ways in favor of upward mobility in the emerging society. Citing Wilson (1959), Gabbert (2001) stated:

30

This was the case, for example, with the funeral ritual that required the sacrifice of cattle. Since this custom involved an investment of both time and stock, kin obligations became incompatible with economic self-interest. The missionaries not only weakened conventional norms but also offered organizational and moral alternatives. Christian villages provided new forms of community based on common faith instead of kinship or economic cooperation. In addition, Christian communities were part of an institution integrating several regions. Thus, migrant workers could find shelter and information among congregations in different places. (p. 302)

Another conflict emerged in the requirement of monogamy as most of the older men were already married to several wives. Though the missionaries disagreed with the practice of polygamy, they accepted the wives for baptism. Another hindrance to conversion was also evident if a man became heir to an older relative; tradition dictated that he was obliged to marry the latter's widow(s). Thus it is not surprising that the majority of converts were female. Citing Wilson (1959), Gabbert (2001) noted that "in the 1930s, women outnumbered men by more than three to two. But what attracted women to Christian congregations and Christian teachings?" (p. 302). The division of Moravian congregations into choirs made it possible for women not only to become full members of the church but also elders, responsible for the women of the congregation. Thus, for the first time women had an opportunity to occupy public positions. "Beyond that, Moravian missionaries advocated the right of women to choose freely whoever they wanted to marry." (Gabbert, 2001, p. 302).

While the missionaries disapproved of Polygyny, it was an acceptable custom to many Africans as it was "a sign of wealth, and highly valued by men." Many wives meant many children. "Sons were desired to help with cultivation and, in pre-colonial times, to act as warriors; Daughters contributed to a man's wealth

31

througn the bride price they brought." The wives were able to assist with agricultural work, the preparation of meals, and the brewing of beer. "Children were the security of their parents in old age, and were expected to pray for them and make offerings after death in order to guarantee them a higher status in the world of their ancestors" (Gabbert, 2001, p. 297).

Gabbert's account of the social groups who were most likely to embrace the missionaries' doctrines, mirrors the arguments of Rambo (1993), and Hoffer (1963) who argued that those on the margins of society will be among the early adopters of new religious ideology. "Missionaries were able to attract people from two Nyakyusa groups in particular: those of a subordinate social position who hoped to improve their status, and individuals who tried to liberate themselves from customary social obligations and from their dependence on older relatives" (Gabbert, 2001, p. 304). In part two of his book, Hoffer (1963) presents seven categories of potential converts: The poor, misfits, the inordinately selfish, the ambitious facing unlimited opportunities, minorities, the bored, and the sinners. In the "poor" category he segments them further as the new poor, the abjectly poor, the free poor, the creative poor, and the unified poor. Hoffer (1963) argued that "though the disaffected are found in all walks of life, they are most frequently in these categories" (p. 26) and it is the poor and frustrated that are easily attracted to new religious ideology.

In Protestant Christianity, everyone can approach God through prayer irrespective of gender, race, age, or class. "This tendency was especially pronounced in Moravian Christianity, which stressed the personal experience of redemption rather than religious doctrine." Christianity was least appealing to the male elders of Nyakyusa because "their status, which depended on polygyny and cattle wealth, was affected by the Christian rule of monogamy and the critical attitude of the missionaries to bride-price payments" (Gabbert, 2001, p. 304).

Missionaries in other regions even fostered what Nutini (1988; as cited in Gabbert, 2001) called "guided syncretism." White Fathers in Ufipa, Tanzania, for example, emphasized the congruence between Fipa religion and Catholicism, and likened ancestral spirits to the angels of Catholic Christianity (Gabbert, 2001, p. 305). Vahakangas (2008) found a similar practice in his study of the Sonjo people of Tanzania. The churches working among the Sonjo consider their success limited at first because of low conversion numbers and especially limited participation in church activities.

According to Potkanski and Adams (1998; as cited in Vahakangas, 2008), the Sonjo or Ba-temi are a Bantu-speaking people based in a semi-arid area of northern Tanzania. Their economy is based on agriculture which is dependent on irrigation. Although the Sonjo people have some similarities in clothing, decorations, weaponry etc. with the Maasai, there is a strong antagonism between both groups. The Sonjo word for Maasai is the same as the word for "enemy." Other distinctions between both groups are these:

> Unlike the Sonjo, the Maasai speak a Nilotic language and are predominantly pastoral. The Sonjo used to live in fortified villages in fear of the Maasai and wild animals. Most of these villages have been abandoned as a result of Ujamaa-socialist forced resettlement programs and the fact that population increases caused the villages to be physically too small. (Vahakangas, 2008, p. 113)

> Each Sonjo village forms an independent entity, and there were no political structures linking Sonjo from different villages. Yet, they had, and still have a strong sense of belonging together. A central dimension of this togetherness, and their identity as "the Sonjo' is their religious heritage. (Vahakangas, 2008, p. 114)

Vahakangas (2008) also pointed out that within each Sonjo village are traditional leaders (*mwenamijie* (singular); *wenamijie* (plural), who control the use of irrigation water, arable land, and the trees. "Because the economy is based on irrigated agriculture, the power over water is the most valuable political power one can have." One of the individuals interviewed in the Vahakangas study (2008) pointed out that "the individual who controls water controls the whole village" (Vahakangas, 2008, p. 114). The traditional leaders make decisions jointly and the position is usually held until death at which time it passes to a successor from within the same clan. "Each village also has a priest, who acts in close cooperation with the wenamijie but he does not have a significant political role" (Vahakangas, 2008, p. 114). The political structure of the clan is gradually being replaced as more emphasis is placed today on the power and influence of elected government officials.

The Lutheran Church began its missionary work among the Sonjo people in 1947. Five years later "an American-led Roman Catholic mission entered the area." The third and latest arrival was the Pentecostal "Church of 72", which is a small and vigorous community active in Digodigo (Vahakangas, 2008, p. 115). As Vahakangas studied the Sonjo people, he discovered that their traditional African religion included a character similar to the Christian Jesus. "Ghambageu, an apotheosized cultural hero, is the most central figure of Sonjo mythology". There exists no standard account of his life, but there are several versions which are as varied as the narrators and the time of narration. Based on the Sonjo age grade list, one can estimate that Ghambageu lived approximately 400 years ago (Vahakangas, 2008, p. 116). The story of the life of Ghambageu is recounted as follows:

> Ghambageu came to the world "automatically", not having a mother or a father. He was a poor man in the village of Tinaga, who worked as a babysitter. He refused to participate in the communal labor of fixing the

34

irrigation channels and also played tricks on the Tinaga inhabitants. The Tinagans grew angry with him and decided to kill him. (p. 117)

Ghambageu got wind of the plot and escaped to the village of Samunge where he performed miracles. He became a hero and a leader, got married and had many children. The myth goes on to say that he had so many children that he could no longer deal with all of them so he decided to turn them into stones except for two of his sons. One of the two sons was later expelled leaving only his favorite son Aka at home. When Aka decided to run away from him he became distraught and moved to the village of Kisangiro where he eventually died (Vahakangas, 2008).

Upon his death, Ghambageu requested "that he should not be buried, but be placed on a flat stone to dry in the sun." The Kisangiro villagers did not comply with his request, and chose instead to bury him. Once the Samunge villagers heard of this they rushed to Kisangiro and opened the grave. "The grave was found to be empty except for Ghambageu's sandals." Thus they believed that he had risen from the dead. Ghambageu is expected to come back at the end of time to save all of the Sonjo people (Vahakangas, 2008, p. 117). There is also another myth of a birth of the son of the sun from a virgin impregnated by a sun ray. The son is sometimes called Ehoru, who would be Ghambageu's grandfather in some versions of the myth. There are variations in the details of this myth, but the main features of the story are the same. In the story, a virgin maiden was bathing in a river when a sunbeam struck her. This sunbeam impregnated her and she gave birth to a son after a very long time (Vahakangas, 2008).

The clan leaders claim that their leadership positions were instated by Ghambageu. Those who question their religious, political, and economic leadership have two avenues available: "either to try to sever the connection between the wenamijie and Ghambageu or to discredit Ghambageu" (Vahakangas,

35

2008, p. 118). The churches have chosen the latter option contending that if Ghambageu became less important, there would be more space for conversions to Christianity. It would also possibly facilitate a gradual separation of religion from politics, which would make the terrain easier and more familiar for the churches. This however, argues Vahakangas (2008), would rob the traditional political leadership of its legitimacy possibly leading to the disintegration of the traditional community. Vahakangas observed that:

> For the Sonjo, Ghambageu is not only a cultural hero, but also a *mugwe*. The traditional meaning of mugwe covers divinities and spirits. The word can also refer to the creator God as well as any other spiritual being. Calling Ghambageu a mugwe can therefore signify many different things. (p. 120)

The Ghambageu story can be seen as an example of syncretism. This allows individuals to mix old and new religious ideologies into a convenient whole, thus creating a third product which has some elements which are the same and others different from their traditional beliefs. This can prove problematic for missionaries who would much rather an abandonment of the old ways for the new ideologies. Syncretism is very common within African societies. The upcoming segment examines this phenomenon in detail.

Syncretism of Traditional African Religion and Christianity

The Pew Research Center (2010), described traditional African religion as follows:

> Handed down over generations, indigenous African religions have no formal creeds or sacred texts comparable to the Bible or Koran. They find expression, instead, in oral traditions, myths, rituals, festivals,

shrines, art and symbols. In the past, Westerners sometimes described them as animism, paganism, ancestor worship or simply superstition, but today scholars acknowledge the existence of sophisticated African traditional religions whose primary role is to provide for human well-being in the present as opposed to offering salvation in a future world. (p. 6)

In general, traditional African religion includes a belief in a supreme being who created and ordered the world but is now somewhat distant from it and often unavailable for direct contact with human beings. Humans are expected however to adhere to the rules and regulations given and any lapse in social responsibilities or violations of taboos will result in hardship, suffering and illness, not only for the culprits, but at times the consequences can be felt by entire communities. These "sins" must be atoned for with ritual acts to re-establish order, harmony and well-being.

Despite the dominance of Christianity and Islam, traditional African religious beliefs and practices have not disappeared. Rather they coexist with Islam and Christianity. Side by side with their high levels of commitment to Christianity and Islam, many people in the countries surveyed by the Pew Research Center retained beliefs and rituals that are characteristic of traditional African religions. In the Pew study (2010) for instance, half or more of the population in at least four countries, including Tanzania, believed that sacrifices to ancestors or spirits would protect them from harm. In addition, roughly a quarter or more of the population in 11 countries said they believed in the protective power of *juju* (charms or amulets), shrines and other sacred objects. In addition to expressing high levels of belief in the protective power of sacrificial offerings and sacred objects, 62% of Tanzanians surveyed, said they believed in the "evil eye", or the ability of certain people to cast malevolent curses or spells (Pew Research Center, 2010, pp. 33, 34).

As explained in the Vahakangas (2008) study, the Sonjo people of Tanzania had succeeded in "Christianizing" Ghambageu by blending some of the parallels between Jesus and Ghambageu. Among these two icons are similarities such as supernatural birth, ability to work miracles, alleged resurrection, as well as the hope of their second advent. Based on interviews conducted during Vahakangas' study (2008), it was noted that the modern Ghambageu list of "dos" and "don'ts" looked very similar to Christian doctrines based on the law presented in the Old Testament (The Bible, Exodus 20), as well as principles taught in New Testament books such as Matthew, Luke, John, and several epistles of the Apostle Paul. Some of the doctrinal similarities included: do not commit adultery, do not kill, do not steal, do not forget the teachings, do everything in prayer, heal the sick in my name, heal the sick by anointing them, in case of trouble pray together and you will receive help, among others. A point of contrast between Sonjo tradition and Christianity is that all three churches in the area (Lutheran, Roman Catholic, and Pentecostal) regard marriage of a divorcee as adultery, whereas divorce and remarriage are an accepted practice within the Sonjo tradition. If the Sonjo people were thus content with their syncretized view of a divine being, what would be the incentive to join another religious group?

Citing Iverson (1984), Vahakangas (2008) explained that a Catholic Father, Gerry Kohler, proposed that the root of the Ghambageu myths must be connected to Jesus in order to facilitate conversion from this traditional belief to Christianity. The Father's theory was intended to present Jesus to the Sonjo in the most acceptable form possible. The proposal appeared to be a failure on the surface, but after closer examination, it became clear that the proposal had a different impact than was expected. It empowered the Sonjo people with the idea that they too could identify Jesus with Ghambageu. Vahakangas (2008) also argued that there still remains the obvious question of whether Ghambageu-Jesus is White or Black,

European or African. One way of solving the problem in a post colonial Tanzania would be to maintain that he is a "mulatto."

Vahakangas (2008) concluded that Sonjo traditional religion was not a wholly passive victim under Christian missionary onslaught, but rather it was an active participant in the creation of a new religious reality. According to Vahakangas (2008), this conclusion is basically in line with the classic intellectual theory of conversion proposed by Horton (1971; as cited in Vahakangas, 2008) which stated that even in the case of change of religious affiliation, the African worldview persists; and while the organizational success of Christian mission has been minimal, the values that the churches have been preaching may well be in surprisingly wide circulation (Vahakangas, 2008, p. 132).

Several of the studies presented on the historical development of Christian missions in various regions of Tanzania, commented on the similarities and differences of Christianity, as brought by the missionaries, and that of traditional African religion already being practiced in those locales. The studies also revealed how both Christianity and traditional religions morphed to create a syncretized religion. Along with the Lutherans, Moravians and Roman Catholics, the Seventh-day Adventists were also engaged in missionary activities in Tanzania during the early 1900s and have documented their experience. Their historic account serves as the final portion of literature reviewed in this chapter.

Adventism in Tanzania

The Tanzania Union Mission was the first to be created in East-Central Africa in 1903 when the first Adventist missionaries arrived there from Germany. The Adventist work began in the north-east region of Tanzania, and extended to the Mara region, the south, then to the west, resulting in the reorganization of the union in 1960. By 1912 the Tanganyika missions had been divided into two general sections – the South Pare Mission Field in the east, and the Victoria Nyanza Mission Field in the West, along the shores of Lake Victoria. Hoschele's work (2007b) featured a map of the Pare region which showed a line distinguishing the area assigned to the Adventists, and that assigned to the Lutherans. Before World War I, each church was assigned its own territory by the government and tried to maintain congenial relations with its neighbors. From 1903-1913 all the SDA mission activities in Tanganyika were supervised by the German Union Conference (Davy, 1963).

The development of Adventism in Tanzania can be divided into five chronological periods, as presented in the centennial publication of Hoschele (2003). "The period of the pioneers" began in 1903 with the first SDA missionaries to Tanganyika (then German East Africa). Waldemar/ Johannes Ehlers and A. C. Enns, arrived there on November 12th. At the time, there was only one small railroad line going from Tanga to Korogwe, a distance of 53 miles. Consequently, travels within most of the country had to be done by foot and thus restricted the missionaries to certain geographic regions. The missionaries used Christian schools as one of their foremost techniques in reaching the people. At first they met strong resistance because of the differing cultural background and language barriers. A breakthrough came as the children grew and embraced the church's teachings on polygamy, smoking, and the use of alcoholic beverages. The first baptism, consisting of six converts was five years in the making. It occurred in Giti in 1908 (Elineema, 1981, 1995).

By 1909 Adventism expanded 20 miles into the lake province where another mission station was established. The Busegwe station later became the headquarters of the Tanzania Union in 1960, and now serves as the headquarters of

40

the Mara Conference. The Majita station, also opened in 1909 declined after the war but was later revived and showed the strongest response to Adventist services. When a school built to hold 160 children was opened in 1910, 600 boys and 175 girls applied (Hoschele, 2007b). As the years went by, the SDA work continued to advance, and three additional districts were established. The faith of the pioneers was so strong that a church with a seating capacity of 600 was built in Majita before anyone was even baptized. This was followed by the translation of the Gospel of Matthew into Chasu, a local language, as well as a hymnal was created with a compilation of Christian songs.

By 1912, F. W. Vasenius, M.D. of Finland became the first SDA physician in Tanganyika (Elineema, 1995). The church's medical work, combined with its educational programs proved very effective in its outreach to the local people, resulting in the largest baptism to date occurring in 1913, when 52 persons were baptized. By 1915, the SDA church was operating 26 schools in Upare, with an enrollment of over 2,000 pupils, and 15 other schools in Victoria Nyanza with an enrollment of over 2,000 pupils as well. During the German era in Tanzania (to 1916) a total of 400 members were baptized (Elineema, 1981).

With the advent of the First World War, the work of the SDA church was left in the hands of native Africans as most of the missionaries vacated the country. Following World War I, the SDA church transitioned to a part African and part British administration and continued to build upon the foundations set by the pioneers. By 1922 the church published a translation of the New Testament in the Pare language and a few years later Africans were ordained as SDA ministers for the first time (Elineema, 1995). The SDA education system experienced a crisis when the Tanzanian government ruled that school attendance was no longer mandatory. Following the ruling, attendance dropped from about 2,000 to only 100 students. To the church's credit however, the college in Suji was able to graduate

41

the first female teacher in Tanzania. Of this accomplishment, the director of education in Tanzania (then Tanganyika) wrote: "Your mission may be justly proud of having established an important landmark in the process of female education" (Elineema, 1981, p. 16).

In less than four decades, the SDA church's membership in Tanzania had grown to more than 3,000 members, with several educational institutions and a medical facility, thus making it necessary for a change in classification, from a mission to a recognized church union. The church's publishing and colporteur (literature evangelist) ministries were also thriving with record numbers in sales of magazines and books. One "Simon of Zanzibar" told an SDA Pastor that he "bought a book six years ago, titled *Wasomaje?* (What Readest Thou?), which was published by the Advent Press. As a result of his discoveries while reading, he became the first person to keep the seventh-day Sabbath in Zanzibar (Masokomya, 1957, p. 10). The printed word became a very significant medium in the growth of the SDA church in Tanzania. More literature evangelists were constantly being trained and sent into un-entered areas. According to Marx (1968), "The Lord was with them, and blessed them abundantly." The letters received from them were encouraging. Their earnest appeal was always the same, "Please send more books the quickest way. The people are waiting for them!"(Marx, 1968, p. 16).

As the work of the literature evangelists became widespread, the church faced a new challenge that of building churches to accommodate the new converts. Elineema (1981) pointed out that land was available free of charge from the local authorities, but it was given on condition that a building would be erected within one year. This therefore meant that the local church would need some financial assistance from the parent organization. Local church leaders lamented the fact that new converts were being lost to other "mission societies" because the pastors had to tell the new believers that the SDA church did not have a place of worship available in their area (Elineema, 1981).

By 1960, the SDA church in Tanzania and Zanzibar had a membership of more than 13, 000 and was organized into its own union "to better facilitate the administration of the rapidly enlarging membership and to meet the changing territorial conditions" (Elineema, 1995). The new organizational structure divided the region into five fields namely: "North East Tanganyika Field (Suji, Tanga, Arusha, and Kilimanjaro regions), Majita-Ukerewe Field (Majita, Ukerewe, and Ururi), West Lake Field (Ntusu, and the region south and west of Lake Victoria), East Lake Field (part of North Mara; Utimbaru), and Tanganyika General Field (the southern half of the country). The last named field included all areas not allocated to the other four fields, and also Zanzibar and Pemba" (Elineema, 1995).

In 1967, the SDA church was able to purchase a property from another denomination that had closed its activities in Arusha, Tanzania (Cook, 1967). This combined with several other facilities in various cities throughout Tanzania helped to confirm that the SDA work was indeed spreading throughout the country. The year 1970 was significant for the work of the SDA church in Tanzania for a number of reasons, first of which was that it was the year of the first Maasai baptisms into the SDA Church. This historic event occurred on February 15th at Suji in the Pare Mountains. The baptismal candidates were three women, "Esther, Lea and Upendo." According to Kisaka (1970a, p. 5), "this harvest was reaped after six long and hard years of labor in Maasailand" (p. 5). Another significant occurrence during this time period was that of the relocation of the church's Tanzanian General Field Headquarters and Radio Department to the city of Morogoro. Henning (1969) reported that within two years, plans were drawn and a building constructed which included "not only the field office but ample space for the Bible Correspondence School and a radio studio" (p. 8).

43

As the work of the SDA church expanded in Tanzania, so did the training of African leadership. John Kisaka became the first Tanzanian SDA pastor to receive a doctorate degree from Andrews University, Michigan, USA, in 1979. "He also became the first principal of the reorganized Tanzania Adventist Seminary and College in 1979, only one year before Yohanna Lusingu was appointed the first African Tanzania Union President" (Hoschele, 2007b, p. 257). The next two decades were characterized by Hoschele (2007b) as a period of rapid growth and new challenges. Several other SDA conferences and mission fields were organized throughout the country and other SDA entities such as ADRA (Adventist Development and Relief Agency) and the International Health Food Association (IHFA) began operations there. The church also began using more international evangelists in face to face as well as satellite evangelism to preach the word in Tanzania. By 2008, the SDA presence in Tanzania was one person in 99 of the general population (Jones & Proctor, 2008).

Within the Tanzania Union Mission today, the SDA Church operates educational institutions, medical facilities, media outlets, churches and other entities within six regional conferences/ fields. The organizational structure from the General Conference of SDA to a local SDA Church is depicted in Figure 1. The five conferences and one field will now be discussed according to their date of initial organization, from the oldest to the youngest. A map of Tanzania showing the administrative regions and the corresponding SDA Conferences/ field is included as Figure 2, to aid our understanding of the various locations. The base map was derived from http://en.wikipedia.org/wiki/Tanzania and the SDA Conference regions were added and the map re-colored for visual impact.

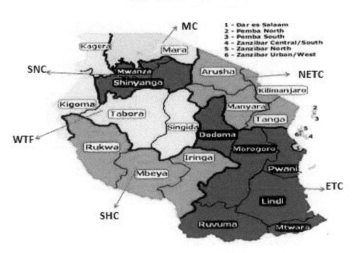

MAP OF TANZANIA

Figure 2: Map of Tanzania showing SDA Conference Regions

North East Tanzania Conference (NETC)

The SDA missionaries arriving from Germany in 1903 established the first SDA mission post within the north east region of Tanzania. Hoschele (2003) cited a map of the region showing the initial distinguishing line between the area assigned to the Adventists, and that assigned to the Lutherans. Today the NETC office is located in Same, Tanzania. As its membership and economic strength increased the NETC was reorganized in 1960 and again in 1990. The 2011 SDA Yearbook estimated the NETC population at seven million, with an SDA membership of a little more than 80 thousand, for a member to population ratio of 1 to 88. Within the NETC are 312 SDA Churches, the University of Arusha,

45

Parane Secondary School, three clinics, and six dispensaries. ADRA also has its regional office within this conference, and has operated the Cradle of Love Baby Home on its compound since 2004 (The Cradle of Love is a home for babies infected with HIV). NETC includes the regions of Arusha, Kilimanjaro, Manyara, and Tanga. In 1967 the SDA Church purchased a property from another denomination which was closing its operations in Arusha. This was a sign of the SDA Church's expansion of activities and membership within the region.

Mara Conference (MC)

The Mara Conference was established in 1909 as the SDA missionaries expanded their work in a north westerly direction into the Lake Victoria area. According to Hoschele (2007b), a school was built in 1910 to accommodate 160 students but when it opened, more than 700 students applied. The Mara region has the smallest population, but the highest SDA member to population ratio of 1:19. The rapid growth of this conference has resulted in it being reorganized six times. Within this conference are 353 SDA Churches, the Ikizu Secondary School, and five SDA dispensaries. In addition to local church initiatives, the SDA Church engages in satellite evangelism along with AWR broadcasts to spread the gospel in this region in the Maasai language.

South Nyanza Conference (SNC)

The SNC was the third SDA Conference to be organized in 1912 (reorganized in 1960, and 1990). This conference covers the region to the immediate west of the NEC, and south of the MC. The church operates four dispensaries in the region and engages in the sale of its print media at the Adventist Book Center (ABC). The church has a member to population ratio of 1:63. There are 584 SDA Churches in the SNC which is the largest number of churches in a TUM Conference. The SNC covers the administrative districts of Mwanza, and Shinyanga. Figure 3 shows the number of SDA Churches in the SNC in comparison to the other SDA conferences in Tanzania. The figure was created based on the statistics available in the SDA Yearbook (2011).

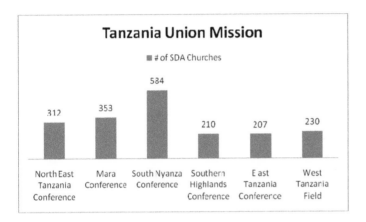

Figure 3: Number of SDA Churches within the Tanzania Union Mission

Southern Highlands Conference (SHC)

The SHC, formerly known as the South West Tanzania Field, was first created in 1960 and reorganized in 1982, 1990, and as recent as 2009 when it changed its status from a mission field to a conference. This status change was a direct outgrowth of "Strategic Issue # 4: Self-Support" as outlined in the East Central Africa Division's Strategic 2003-2010 Plan. The plan had as one of its priorities, enabling its mission fields (dependence status) to become a conference (self-supporting status). This was made possible by an increase in the percentage of tithe and offerings collected within the region. The SDA Church operates three dispensaries within this conference. The SHC encompasses the districts of Iringa, Mbeya, and Rukwa.

East Tanzania Conference (ETC)

The ETC is the largest geographic region of the TUM conferences and covers the districts of Dodoma, Lindi, Morogoro, Mtwara, Pwani, and Ruvuma regions, along with the islands of Pemba and Unguja. The SDA church has the second lowest SDA member to population ratio within this conference (1:202), despite having the AWR studio in Morogoro as well as the Tanzania Adventist Press, two health service facilities and five dispensaries. The low SDA member to population ratio serves as a constant reminder that conversion is a process which occurs through channels and advocates in a social system, over time. Other factors worth considering are that this conference is home to both the commercial and legislative capitals of Tanzania.

West Tanzania Field (WTF)

The WTF was created in 1990 and encompasses the regions of Kagera, Kigoma, Singida and Tabora. Within this field, the SDA Church operates seven dispensaries, and the only SDA hospital in Tanzania: The Heri Adventist Hospital. There are 230 SDA Churches in the WTF, with an SDA membership of 42 thousand, in a population of 8.5 million. This equates to a member to population ratio of 1:203. This therefore places the WTF within the priority broadcast region of AWR. The SDA Church also engages in satellite evangelism within this field.

In the words of Elineema (1981), the story of Adventism in Tanzania is a story of the triumph of faith. The church's expansion in this country came about "under God's blessing and the cooperation and joint efforts of missionaries, indigenous workers, and laity" (p. 17). The 25 year period under the purview of this study has experienced growth and challenges. Tanzania Union Mission is now one of the leading divisions of the SDA church in East Central Africa. It is projected that the church's membership will continue to increase as various agencies and ministries pool their resources together to fulfill the church's mission.

CHAPTER 3: REVIEW OF LITERATURE

This review of literature encompasses several subject areas including the historical context of international religious broadcasting, radio usage and media effects studies done in Africa, theories of religion such as those advocated by Karl Marx (1974), and Emile Durkheim (1912), the process of religious conversion, and previous research utilizing the Diffusion of Innovations theory (Rogers, 2003). These intersecting fields of study weave together a rich backdrop for the current study as it brings together religion, mass communication, and media studies. First to be examined is the origins of religious broadcasting.

Origins of Religious Broadcasting

On January 2, 1921, just two months to the day after the first US radio broadcast, KDKA aired the first religious service from a church in Pittsburgh, PA, USA (Christian History Institute, 2007). It was undertaken by Westinghouse, an electric company which owned the pioneer Pittsburg station KDKA (Head, Sterling & Schofield, 1994). The goal was to test its ability to do a remote broadcast far from the radio studio. Pittsburgh's Calvary Episcopal Church was chosen because one of the Westinghouse engineers happened to be a member of the choir and made the arrangements. Since then, religious radio broadcasts have been developed and transmitted, not just far from the radio studio, but even across international terrain. According to Leonard (2003), established churches always had something to say, and often had charismatic individuals who could say it well over the wireless system.

50

Today, radio is a powerful medium used by many entities, including religious organizations desirous of reaching "behind the lines in nations where preaching the gospel is not allowed" (Christian History Institute, 2007). Radio knows no walls or fences, says Hale (1975) who went on to describe it as "the only unstoppable medium of mass communication" (p. ix). It is radio's special function to penetrate even where it is not wanted, even reaching audiences whose governments would rather they were not reached (Hale, 1975). This dimension of radio has made it a popular vehicle for many religious denominations to utilize in the fulfillment of their mission. There are several international religious broadcasters (IRB) currently utilizing this medium around the globe, most of which have their headquarters in the United States of America. Chapter one of this study outlined the historical development of one such IRB known as Adventist World Radio (AWR). Now will be examined, the historical development of the realm of international religious broadcasting, years before the inception of AWR.

History of International Religious Broadcasting

The first international religious broadcaster was Station HCJB (Heralding Christ Jesus Broadcasting) which went on the air in 1931 in Quito, Ecuador. Stoneman (2006) employed a historical analysis to trace the development of global Christian media, through a close examination of the activities of Station HCJB. Considered as the "Pioneer Missionary Broadcaster," HCJB has played an important role in the spread of the evangelical doctrines throughout Latin America. It established broadcast practices that served as a model in the emerging field of missionary radio after WWII.

For over 20 years HCJB remained the only international radio station dedicated to transmitting the gospel to foreign audiences. By the mid 1950s, there were 16 conservative religious broadcasters covering the globe on medium wave

51

and shortwave, with stations in Central and South America, the Caribbean, much of Asia, West Africa, North Africa and Europe (Stoneman, 2007). The 1974 edition of the *World Radio and TV Handbook*, listed 40 separate religious broadcasting organizations. Seven worldwide operations were based in the United States, namely: Adventist World Radio, Trans World Radio, the Evangelical Alliance Mission, the West Indies Mission, the Far East Broadcasting Company Inc. (from Manila), World Radio Gospel Hour, and the Herald of Truth Broadcast (Hale, 1975). Today, there are hundreds of religious broadcasting operations around the world including African pioneers ELWA (Eternal Love Winning Africa) from Liberia (ELWA Ministries, 2008). But despite the growing trend of missionaries utilizing radio to spread a religious message, not much research has been conducted in this regard (Kushner, 1976; Hughes, 1980). Some of the research that have been done include media effects studies focused on the effectiveness of various educational, political, and entertainment-education programs. A few of these studies will now be highlighted.

Radio Usage and Media Effects in Africa

Media scholars tend to agree that media effects are difficult to measure (Korzenny, & Schiff, 1992; Sparks, 2006). Traditionally, most media effects studies were done quantitatively, but there are equally viable qualitative methods for studying media effects. According to Sparks (2006), a quantitative researcher needs to fulfill at least three criteria in order to prove that the media affected the audience in a particular way. The first criterion that the researcher needs to establish is that the two things in question – a media message, and a change in attitude or behavior - are empirically related to each other. Secondly, in order to

52

clearly establish causality, the time order of the two variables must be such that researchers can safely document that the independent variable acts upon the dependent variable to cause an effect. Once empirical relationships and time-order have been established, a researcher must then demonstrate that the observed relationship is not due to some unmeasured variable casually related to both of the others.

In addition to the criteria mentioned above, Chaffee (1992) argued that it is important for researchers to specify their theory of what is static and what is changing. A media effect is believed to have occurred when "a change in the media, such as a new channel or novel content, is introduced and a subsequent change is observed in members of the audience" (Chaffee, 1992, p. 39). The task of theory therefore is to specify the linkage between these two changes. From a methodological perspective, this type of change model corresponds to a laboratory experiment, where a manipulation (change in media) is performed, and then the hypothesized outcomes (changes in person) are measured. It is difficult however to create the optimal experiment when working with human subjects as it is not always possible to control all intervening variables. The experiment is the least often utilized method of the options available to media researchers. The more frequently used methods include content analysis and surveys. Qualitative methods include interviews, ethnography, textual analysis and the historical systematic methodology.

Studies have been conducted, documenting how radio has been used, as well as the media effect of various radio broadcasts. In a previous review of literature undertaken by this researcher, several studies were identified in the Americas, Asia, Europe and Africa. These studies occurred in different parts of the world but there was an underlining theme, that of radio being a pervasive medium. Most of the articles reviewed focused on radio usage and its impact, with the researcher's

53

purpose at the time being that of understanding the role that radio played in bringing about social change (Vernon, 2009).

Several of the articles reviewed included studies conducted in Africa, namely in countries such as Chad (Perry, 2003); Ghana (De Witte, 2003); Kenya (Ligaga, 2005); Madagascar (Razafimbelo-Harisoa, 2005); Rwanda (Straus, 2007); Tanzania (Vaughan & Rogers, 2000); Uganda (Santora, 1997); Zambia (Spitulnik, 2000) and Zimbabwe (Mano, 2004). These studies can be divided into categories: those focusing on radio as a vehicle for entertainment-education, politically oriented programming, and religious radio stations. A portion of these studies is presented in brief.

Radio as a Medium of Entertainment and Education

Singhal and Rogers' study (as cited in Ligaga, 2005), and Vaughan and Rogers (2000), explained entertainment education as the process of creating broadcast programs with the following intentional outcomes in the audience: "increase audience members' knowledge about an issue, create favorable attitudes, shift social norms, and change overt behavior of individuals and communities" (Ligaga, 2005, p. 134). An example of a program created to achieve the dual purpose of entertainment and education, was that of the radio talk program *Chakafukidza* (Mano, 2004). *Chakafukidza* is a Shona term which refers to the secrecy that adults in most societies often attach to domestic affairs and personal problems. The Zimbabwe Broadcasting Corporation (ZBC) used this radio talk program to address issues that were often difficult to deal with in face-to-face discussions. For two decades (1981-2001), the producers capitalized on the radio medium as a contemporary way to reconstitute a technological "*dare* in response to the fast collapsing age-old practices within the Shona society" (Mano, 2004, p.

54

319). Traditionally, the dare was a local same-sex gathering for those who were married, widowed, or contemplating marriage. The older members of the village were seen as the advisors to the younger members of the group. The radio dare, initially featured the reading of letters from listeners, and an in-studio panel of advisors addressing the marital issues presented by the listeners in their correspondences. After five years on the air, the *Chakafukidza* program incorporated a telephone call-in segment which allowed for more audience participation within the program.

One of the challenges encountered with the radio medium was that it could not guarantee the separation of the sexes, or the exclusion of listeners who were not of marriageable age. Consequently, the program was broadcast between 8:30 p.m. and 9:30 p.m., and the producers issued a warning at the beginning of each program. The warning was a signal for listeners to regroup if they felt that they were in "polite company" and would be embarrassed to discuss marital issues with those listening nearby. The producers felt that the radio program was a success because it brought together dispersed individuals. With the radio broadcast, listeners were no longer restricted to the dare within their local village, but they could be exposed to other perspectives from diverse locations. The radio dare thus "decreased the significance of physical presence in the experience of people and events" (Mano, 2004, p. 323).

Another example of radio being used for entertainment-education was identified in Ligaga's study (2005). The Kenyan radio drama *Ushikwapo Shikamana* sought to invite listeners to apply the lessons and themes of the broadcasts, to their daily lives. In *Ushikwapo Shikamana* (if assisted, assist yourself), the Kenya Broadcasting Corporation (KBC) sought to present, in a public forum, the effects of HIV/AIDS and female circumcision. Though its initial time on the air was relatively short due to a lack of funds, it was returned to the

55

airwaves because of its effectiveness. The radio drama usually unfolded in three zones: a rural space, a peri-urban area and the urban centre. It often juxtaposed traditional activities with contemporary circumstances.

Theorists of radio have indicated that radio drama as a genre depends on the interaction of sound and a listener's imagination. In a process labeled as transcodification (Ligaga 2005, p. 135), radio relies on images previously known or identifiable to listeners on a visual level and utilizes sound to try and capture the same image in a way that can easily be decoded by the listeners. Radio drama is thus a medium which requires relatively high levels of listener participation, unlike the pure music format which can be enjoyed as background listening. Listenership studies on *Ushikwapo Shikamana,* conducted by Singhal and Rogers (2003), indicated that the play was extremely popular with Kenyan audiences. More than 800 episodes were broadcasted since the program resumed in 1998. One estimate was that 56 % of Kiswahili speakers tuned in to the play on a bi-weekly basis.

In Tanzania, radio is also the most appropriate channel for broadcasting an entertainment-education program to a mass audience. Vaughan and Rogers (2000), conducted a study in Tanzania (1993-1997), which examined the communication effects of an entertainment-education radio soap opera called *Twende na Wakati* (Let's Go With the Times). The program was produced by Radio Tanzania, in conjunction with other agencies such as: the Tanzanian Ministry of Health; Population Communication International (PCI), (a nongovernmental organization headquartered in New York that provided technical assistance on the entertainment-education strategy); and the UNFPA [United Nations Population Fund], that provided much of the funding. The purpose of the radio soap opera was to entertain and educate the Tanzanian population about the harmful consequences of rapid population growth, and to encourage the listeners to adopt a family planning method. The episodes of the radio drama were created locally in Tanzania as a means of ensuring that the content was culturally sensitive.

The program aired for 30-minutes, two times per week, for two years throughout the country, with the exception of one region, Dodoma, which was used as the control group. Vaughan and Rogers' (2000) data consisted of approximately 2700 interviews conducted yearly for five years (including a pre-broadcast survey done in 1993), in 35 pre-designated regions. Appropriate measures were taken to ensure that the random, yet purposive sample included equal numbers of men and women each year from each region. Vaughan and Rogers (2000) used multiple theories, namely (1) the hierarchy-of-effects model, (2) the stages-of-change model, (3) social learning theory, and (4) the diffusion of innovations (DOI), to establish their framework which synthesized a six-stage model depicting the way in which communication messages have contributed to individual behavior change. The stages of the Vaughan & Rogers' (2000) model are: (1) Pre-contemplation (2) Contemplation (3) Preparation (4) Validation (5) Action, and (6) Maintenance. Stages two and three are divided into two parts with part "A" referring to cognitive processes, and part "B" dealing with affective processes. The study's findings are summarized as follows.

The Vaughan and Rogers' study (2000) revealed that most of the listeners were familiar with family planning methods prior to listening to the radio drama, and 71% of the survey respondents could name at least one family planning method without being prompted. Thus a very small percentage of the sample was assigned to the first stage. About 10% of the respondents were categorized as being in the contemplative stage during the first year of the study. This percentage also declined as the study progressed. Ninety-seven percent of the listeners in the sample recognized the governments and the Ministry of Health's agenda of educating the population about family planning methods and agreed that something needed to be done. Many of the listener correspondences submitted to Radio Tanzania contained "calls to action" for the lead female character, Tunu (the wife of Mkwaju). Listeners were instructing her to take charge of her life and to adopt family planning (Vaughan & Rogers, 2000, p. 216).

The preparation stage included 10% of the sample and consisted of respondents who approved of family planning and believed that it was possible to determine one's own family size. This group also included those who had shared with a friend, their intention to adopt a family planning method. The validation stage was comprised of 10-20% of the respondents who had talked to their spouse/partner about family planning. Vaughan and Rogers (2000), noted that "spousal communication and joint decision making were emphasized in 63% of the 205 episodes of the radio soap opera during the first two years of broadcasts" (p. 217). The Vaughan and Rogers' study (2000) also found a positive correlation between spousal communication about family planning, and contraceptive use in Tanzania. They found that a "lack of discussion was more likely to lead to an individual wrongly concluding that his spouse is opposed to family planning, thereby proving a block to the adoption of family planning" (p. 218). The radio soap opera was credited for successfully promoting discussions among couples who were persuaded to emulate the leading characters in the soap opera who frequently spoke about such matters.

Stage five is the action stage, and it accounted for 10-30% of the respondents in the sample. Respondents were assigned to this category if "they were currently "sometimes" users of a family planning method, or (2) they reported that they had "ever used" a family planning method, or (3) they had discussed family planning with a family planning worker" (p. 218). The sixth and final classification of respondents was those in the maintenance stage. This group consisted of those who reported that a family planning method was always used by at least one spousal partner. This stage was the largest category in number of respondents, and it also showed an increase in the treatment area as the longitudinal study progressed. In 1995, 22% of *Twende na Wakati* listeners reported that they adopted family planning as a result of listening to the radio soap opera. By 1997, this population increased to 70 % thus showing a significant increase. The findings of the Vaughan and Rogers' (2000) study were supported by data collected from 49 Ministry of Health Clinics in the broadcast area, which reported a 20% increase in new family planning adopters.

The preceding studies have shown radio as a successful instrument in Africa, to broadcast information packaged as entertainment-education. Not only is radio being used in this way, but as the following studies indicate, radio is also used as a means to promote and or decry political agendas.

Politically Oriented Programming

Uganda has had a long history of government owned and operated radio stations until the airwaves opened up to private stations in 1995. Sanyu Radio became the first private station to broadcast from the capital city of Kampala. One year later Capital Radio appeared, and moved beyond the entertainment-only format to a dual one of entertainment and education of its citizens. To date the Ugandan capital of Kampala has more operational radio stations than Tanzania and Kenya combined (Uganda web, 2005). The most popular theme of the Ugandan talk radio programs is that of criticizing the government. During the two-hour show "Capital Gang," callers and commentators are free to voice their support for, or their disfavor of government initiatives, as well as their personal biases about specific politicians. One talk show host remarked that he never had any personal issues with the government, but whenever a cabinet minister or a member of

59

parliament does something stupid, he will "go straight for the jugular" (Santoro, 1997, p. 7).

Not only is radio used to criticize the government, as is the case in Uganda, but in the neighboring country of Rwanda, the court maintained that hate radio "played an essential role" in the Rwandan genocide of 1994 by "indirectly and directly inciting listeners to commit genocidal violence" (Strauss, 2007, p. 614). Strauss argued however that despite very strong causal claims about media effects commonly found in commentary on Rwanda, the supporting evidence was weak. His study acknowledged that there were examples where RTLM (Radio-Television Libre des Milles Collines) had broadcast specific names and places, which were followed by attacks on those individuals and locations. Strauss (2007) concluded that the cases in which radio was directly linked to genocidal acts comprised only a tiny fraction of the total violence that occurred, and that the radio station's influence was limited to the capital and its immediate surroundings.

While the use of radio to incite hateful and violent acts in the Rwandan genocide remains questionable, the potential of radio as a tool for peace and reconciliation was being explored successfully in Chad and Niger. Perry (2003) described her observations and experience as a guest speaker for the US government's Africa Regional Services Program. A part of her responsibilities included traveling throughout francophone Africa to conduct workshops on mediation and conflict resolution. During each of her two missions to Chad in 2002, Perry followed up her workshop discussions with airtime on the community radio stations. One of the metaphors she utilized is that of the hippopotamus under water. This imagery is used to discuss "the seething conflict in the region – hidden enemies, submerged meanings, and a general unwillingness to name the sources of conflict" (Perry, 2003, p. 561). Perry argued that radio can play a key role in luring the hippopotamus out of the water to size up the true shape and complexity of ongoing conflict. Radio has always played a major development role in Africa and within the past decade it has begun to figure prominently in peace consolidation across the continent.

The Freeplay Foundation was cited by Perry for "having worked extensively with the United Nations and other nongovernmental organizations to provide solar-powered radios to conflict victims throughout Africa – from orphans in Rwanda to flood victims in Mozambique" (Perry, 2003, p. 562). Chad has adopted the solar-powered radios for guns exchange program, which was modeled after a similar program in Niger. In a highly integrated program managed by the Nigerien government and funded in part by the United Nations Development Program Trust Fund for the Prevention and Reduction of the Proliferation of Small Arms, the thriving network of community radio stations has begun the shift to solar-powered generators, while local residents are being trained as announcers, producers, journalists, and station managers. Perry noted that women and children especially, had come to value the information provided on the radio, as their most cherished possession in their quest for personal safety.

A study done in the country of Madagascar adds another component to the use of radio to present politically oriented programming. Razafimbelo-Harisoa (2005), argued that in Madagascar, radio was a real social intervention medium and a vehicle for propaganda among younger politicians. Most politicians typically launched their personal stations to promote their own agendas and criticize that of their opponents during an election campaign, but the political radio stations are usually short lived and tend to die out after the election process is completed. Razafimbelo-Harisoa (2005) offered several examples of political stations such as MBS (the Madagascar Broadcasting System), which belonged to President Marc Ravalomanana (he also owned a local newspaper); and other stations owned by elected officials such as former government ministers and mayors.

In Madagascar not only do political stations play a significant role, but approximately one third of the 200 stations in existence were geared towards religious programming. In Madagascar, the tendency is for the religious organization to own the stations, while in Ghana the trend is to purchase primetime spots for religious broadcasts.

Religious Radio Programming

According to Razafimbelo-Harisoa (2005), religious stations occupy a significant place in the Malagasy radio landscape. There are 71 of them among the 200 listed private radio stations on the island. They are characterized by the prominence of religious programs, and are funded in part by their congregations. The most powerful religious station in Madagascar is RDB (Radio Don Bosco), a Catholic station launched in 1996. The program content usually includes educational programming, music, entertainment, news, call-in programs, with 25% of the content being religious. RDB also transmits live and unedited Radio Vatican programming related to the African continent. Razafimbelo-Harisoa (2005) cautiously noted an interesting union of religion and politics: The Federation of the Christian Church in Madagascar consisted of Catholics, Protestants and Anglicans and this organization was very active during the political events of 1991 and 2002. It was even believed that the support of the Church Federation seemed to be an effective electoral guarantee and an alliance in that direction was a sensible electoral strategy.

While the radio stations in Ghana are not identified as "politically oriented", or "religious" stations, De Witte (2003) observed that many of the new private FM radio stations there are owned by "born-again Christians" and this greatly influences the programming.　　De Witte quoted a religious leader from Ghana who stated that churches are keeping the radio stations in business by paying for interviews, advertisements, and airtime. The religious leader saw his church's contribution as "significant to national development, as religious broadcasts have become the bedrock of the media industry in the country" (De Witte, 2003, p. 177).

According to De Witte (2003), until 1992, the media in Ghana had been largely controlled by the state. After the turn to democracy rule in 1992, the Ghanaian state loosened control over the media, thus giving way to a rapidly evolving private media scene. Religious programming accounted for a large percentage of airtime on most of the FM radio stations and on weekends a series of church services and sermons filled five hours of television time. The De Witte study focused on the broadcast operations of the International Central Gospel Church (ICGC) which at the time had more than 100 branches worldwide and was headquartered in Accra, Ghana. De Witte described ICGC as one of the largest and most influential charismatic churches in Ghana. Its Accra site had a church which seated 4,000 individuals, and a weekly prime time TV program with simultaneous radio broadcasts. The founder, and general overseer of ICGC, Mensa Otabil, was quoted as saying that "his church is strongly committed to the development of the country." He propagated what he called practical Christianity and aimed to make the Bible an effective "tool for life" for everybody. Hailed as the "teacher of the nation," it is estimated that ICGC broadcasts have listening audiences of more than two million, with listeners and viewers being of different religions including Muslims, and Christians of different churches, with audience members as far away as Kenya (De Witte, 2003, p. 180, 183, 193).

The impact of the ICGC broadcasts was documented by way of interviews and participant observations. De Witte (2003) found that many people viewed 6 p.m. on Sundays as a special time and they consciously sat down to watch the program. Many even "lock their door" to ensure that they were not disturbed

63

during that time. De Witte also had the opportunity to observe activities at the correspondence office where it was reported that the *Living Word* broadcasts received about 400 listener correspondences each month (De Witte, 2003, p. 194). Some listeners requested audiotapes/ books, while others shared how the programs impacted their lives with the core values of independence, human dignity and excellence.

Laswell (1948), Wright (1960), and McQuail (1984), identified five functions of the mass media: Surveillance, correlation, cultural transmission, entertainment and mobilization (as cited in Infante, Rancer & Womack, 1997). It is clear from the literature reviewed that radio is still very instrumental in fulfilling its mass media functions today. There is still room for further assessment however, as to its effectiveness as a medium for transmitting religious doctrines with the goal of listener conversion from one religious faith to another. Before that assessment is undertaken however, three foundational theories of religion will be presented.

Theories of Religion

Religion is a set of beliefs which surround the role of one or more supernatural beings capable of orchestrating the believer's day to day life (Robertson, 1970, as cited in Haralambos & Holborn, 1990). This belief in the supernatural exists in every culture with varying degrees of emphasis. There are multiple perspectives on religion. Most applicable to this study are three perspectives as set forth by Emile Durkheim (1912), Karl Marx (1974), and Peter Burger and Thomas Luckmann (1969; as cited in Haralambos & Holborn, 1990).

The Functionalist Perspective

Durkheim (1912), (as cited in Haralambos & Holborn, 1990), argued that all societies divided the world into two categories: "the sacred" and "the profane" or non-sacred. This distinction was understood within the culture and agreed upon by the majority. Interactions with the profane were sometimes sanctioned and regulated as a cultural taboo. In collective worship experiences, the members of the culture would gather to celebrate their shared beliefs, express their faith and strengthen their communal bonds. Malinowski (1954) added that "life crises such as birth, puberty, marriage and death are surrounded with religious ritual" (as cited in Haralambos & Holborn, 1990, p. 649). Other theorists of religion such as Talcott Parsons (1965), believed that "religious beliefs give meaning to life; they answer man's questions about himself and the world he lives in" (as cited in Haralambos & Holborn, 1990, p. 652). The main function therefore of religion, is to help mankind understand the world in which we live. Of such is the functionalist perspective in brief.

The Marxist Perspective

The second theory of religion being examined is that of the Marxist Perspective. Marx (1974) viewed religion as "an illusion which eases the pain produced by exploitation and oppression" (as cited in Haralambos & Holborn, 1990, p. 652). Marx blamed religion for its role in keeping the oppressed in their place and not seeking to challenge the dominant ideology that keeps them subjugated. He believed religion to be a drug, "the opium of the people," which numbs the user and dulls their sense of reality. Four of the ways Marx believed that religion dulls "the pain of oppression" are as follows: (1) Christians endure hardship on earth because they believe there is a better life after death. (2) Some religions place a high value on suffering and believe that those who suffer will be richly rewarded. (3) Most religions involve the supernatural, therefore instead of trying to solve life's problems by themselves; adherents tend to believe that there will be divine intervention. (4) Religion allows for a certain level of acceptance and tolerance of life as is, as there is the belief that in time, all wrongs will be made right. Karl Marx's stance is probably the most well known of the three religious viewpoints being presented. Burger and Luckmann (1969), though not as popular as Karl Marx, also provide another valid perspective.

The Phenomenological Perspective

Burger and Luckmann (1969) put forth the phenomenological perspective of religion. They believed that "religion is produced by members of society subjectively interpreting and giving meaning to the world around them" (as cited in Haralambos & Holborn, 1990, p. 656). Those who believe in religion do not usually question aspects that are faith-based. "Things are real because people believe they are real; Life is meaningful because of the meaning people give to it" (as cited in Haralambos & Holborn, 1990, p. 657). The process of religious conversion is also a phenomenon. Each religious group determines what kind of change needs to be evident for conversion to take place.

The work of Rambo (1993) forms the theoretical framework of this study along with that of Rogers (2003). Rambo listed seven stages in a systematic model of conversion. The stages are: context, crisis, quest, encounter, interaction, commitment, and consequences. The first three stages of Rambo's model can be likened to an attribute in the Diffusion of Innovations theory, known as "inner innovativeness" which deals with all the factors that would influence an individual's desire to pursue a new set of religious beliefs. The stages outlined by

Rambo (1993), along with tenets of the Diffusion of Innovation theory form the theoretical framework for this study and will now be examined further.

Theoretical Framework

The process of religious conversion

According to Rambo (1993), "conversion is rarely an overnight, all-in-an-instant, wholesale transformation that is now and forever" (p. 1). Conversion, like diffusion, is a process that is mediated through people, places, and things. Religious conversion can be defined by a religious group and each group determines what kind of change needs to be evident for conversion to be noted as occurring. For Adventists, a request for baptism is a sign of a convert's intention to commit to the faith. Likewise a request for enrollment in a Bible correspondence course could be interpreted as the seeker being a potential convert.

Rambo created a systematic stage model of conversion which takes place in seven stages. In the first stage Rambo (1993) stressed that "conversion takes place within a dynamic context" (p. 20). There is a macro-context which includes national and international forces, and there is the micro-context which focuses on the local setting. The micro-context includes factors such as access to transportation, trade, and military or religious personnel originating in other locales. Muslim and Communist countries such as Sudan and China were cited as having very strict laws against conversion from the state religion. In some cases the punishment was execution hence it is difficult for missionaries to work in those regions.

Duke and Johnson (1989) formulated a macro-sociological theory of

67

religious change. They argued that religious movements develop through a cycle which involves dominance, growth, peak, decline and apostasy. Conversion is most likely during the dominance stage as opposed to the decline and apostasy stages. Rambo (1993) identified several contextual factors which are often prevalent whenever conversion occurs. The first is that of a person or group feeling attached to a religious community. The second occurs when the individual embraces the rituals and traditions of the religious group; and thirdly, the individual experiences a transformation in their worldview or frame of reference such that they now interpret life events as other members of the same religious community would view them. The fourth element Rambo puts forth as a contextual clue occurs when the individual's entire life's purpose is guided by the rules and regulations of the newly embraced religious community. Rambo (1993) points out as well that we usually hear of the thousands of new converts in a given context but we rarely hear of the thousands who resisted or rejected conversion.

The degree of compatibility between the tenets of the new religion and that of the existing religion will also influence the nature of the conversion process. Rambo (1993) proposed multiple hypotheses about the dynamics of conversion. Three of them are as follows: (1) "Indigenous cultures that are stable, resilient, and effective will have few people receptive to conversion." (1.2) "A strong culture will reward conformity and punish deviance"; (2) "Indigenous cultures that are in crisis will have more potential converts than stable societies" (p. 41). The latter hypothesis forms the basis of the second stage of the conversion process. Rambo (1993) argues that "some form of crisis usually precedes conversion...the crisis may be religious, political, psychological, or cultural in origin" (p. 44). The crisis could also be of a personal religious nature as is the case when an individual feels convicted of wrong doing, acknowledges himself or herself as "a sinner," and embraces conversion as a means to the "Savior."

Rambo (1993) discussed the different types of crises, pointing out that some could be in the form of prolonged suffering, sickness, or it could be sudden or tragic such as accidental death. In order to determine the severity of the crisis, Rambo sets forth a continuum which measures, intensity: from mild to severe; duration: from brief to prolonged; scope: from limited to extensive; source: from internal to external; and nature, whether old or new: from continuity to discontinuity (p. 47). For some individuals, the catalyst could be a near death experience, a mystical experience, sickness, death, or a quest for meaning and or transcendence. This quest for something better, leads the individual to the third stage of the conversion process.

Rambo (1993) identified five modes of response often exhibited by individuals going through the quest stage of religious conversion. The first he described as "active questing." In this stage a person is adventurous, and takes the initiative to seek out new ways of being or doing in an attempt to alleviate the pain or dissatisfaction of the old ways. A second mode of response is that of being "receptive." In this case, the individual is not going in search of innovative ways and ideas, but the person is open to considering new options as they present themselves. The third mode of response is "rejecting": the individual makes a deliberate decision to reject the new ideas being presented. As an alternative, the individual could also choose to be "apathetic" which means they will not display any interest in what the new religion has to offer; or a "passive" response mode could be used in which the individual is so desperate for a change that they are vulnerable to all new suggestions from external sources (p. 59).

In the context of religious conversion, external sources could be that of missionaries, and other influencers working on behalf of foreign entities. Some of these influencers are career missionaries, others engage in short term missionary activities, but the motive is usually the same: that of seeking new converts to their religious faith. The outreach activities may be in the form of medical facilities, educational institutions, or other forms of development and relief initiatives. These "inducements" prompted Rambo (1993) and other scholars to question the sincerity of missionary endeavors as well as the sincerity of the converts during the stages of encounter and interaction. Some of the questions raised are as follows: "Do people convert to Christianity because they are convinced of the truth of its message, or because they see it as a route to better technology, improved health care, advanced education, or access to the colonial powers in charge of their area? There is no clear cut answer as the truth involves a combination of factors.

In the encounter phase of Rambo's conversion process, the focus is on the advocate's strategy. The term advocate is used synonymously with missionary, and in this stage one examines the ways in which missionaries carry out their objectives. Some missionaries engage in a "systems-oriented strategy" in which several missionaries will enter a community and "seek to persuade large numbers of people, especially community leaders" to accept the new religious beliefs. An alternative strategy is that of the "concentrated or personalistic" approach which focuses on individuals who are already on the fringes of their community and would be more susceptible to conversion initiatives that offer them a better way of life (Rambo, 1993, p. 79).

Some missionaries engage in face to face interactions while others utilize the media. Some can be very innovative in their approaches to "friendship evangelism" while others adhere to more traditional forms of witnessing such as revival meetings and mass mailings. Rambo (1993) argued that "understanding the human predicament and the origin and destiny of the world is a powerful incentive for people to convert" (p. 82). This is somewhat similar to the functionalist perspective of religion discussed earlier. Individuals are trying to make sense of the world and their experiences, hence any religious system that seeks to provide logical explanations will be attractive to many. Religious groups that provide "techniques for living" are also seen as attractive. Such techniques could include how and when to pray, morning and evening worship with meditational literature as well as other practical applications of religious tenets. The religious group's zeal towards evangelism will also drive how much time and money is spent towards reaching and retaining new converts.

The actual interactions between the missionary and the potential convert are considered a separate stage in the conversion process. In an effort to strengthen their influence in a given community, some missionaries established self-contained compounds including schools, churches, hospitals and stores, to foster a clear distinction between those who are adherents of the new religion and those who are not. Rambo (1993) characterized these self-contained communities as a part of an "encapsulation" strategy but argued that this procedure is not unique to religious bodies. He argued that "every classroom is a form of encapsulation in that it creates an environment in which there can be concentration on the topic at hand, control of noise and competing ideas, and minimal interruption" (Rambo 1993, p. 104). Often the resources available within the compounds are more advanced and therefore more attractive, thus enticing others to join the new religious community.

The goal of these encounters is to build trust, strengthen relationships, and make disciples who will in turn share their testimonies with others. Rambo believes that these encounters provide benefits for both parties. The missionaries, for example, "gratify spiritual, educational, and health-care needs, and the converts in return give attention, attendance, and adherence to the new religious belief system" (Rambo 1993, p. 113). In this stage of the conversion process, rituals are very important. They serve to separate believers from unbelievers, help in the assimilation process, and often help to solidify the new religious ideas in the minds of the new converts. Some of the rituals employed by Protestant groups include

71

baptism by emersion, communion, fasting and prayer.

The sixth stage of Rambo's conversion process is that of commitment. The rituals introduced in the previous stage are now reinforced and the new convert engages in a public declaration of their decision to forsake the old ways and to embrace a new way of life. This stage involves sharing the testimony of their transformation, and learning the jargon of the new religion. The convert is expected to practice the inner commitment of total surrender to a divine power. During this stage of the process, conflict and crises often arise. The convert may feel a sense of loss when contemplating the family or community ties that were severed, in comparison to the new ties established within the new religious community. Rambo contends that this "inner resolve to shift loyalties is never complete; Old urges return, sometimes with greater power than before" (p. 136). Religious groups that make allowances for these post decision conflicts tend to retain more of their members as opposed to more conservative groups that expect the old ways to die and remain buried.

The final stage in Rambo's (1993) conversion process is "consequences." In the 1980s for example, Nepal had Hinduism as the state religion and it was unlawful for anyone to convert from Hinduism. Those who accepted Christian baptism were given a one year prison term, and the one who administered the baptism was liable for a seven year term (Kane, 1981). Today, the laws are not as stringent, but some stigma remains. Wherever a religion is strongly entrenched, people tend to identify with that religion. Job opportunities and other benefits may depend on it. Scragg and Steele (1996) recounted the story of Lwin who was driven from her home when she refused to denounce her new found Christian faith. The other members of her community pressured her parents, and accused them of bringing a curse on the village. This societal pressure drove Lwin to attempt suicide twice (Scragg & Steele, 1996).

Some of the positive consequences cited by Rambo (1993) were based on Turner's (1979) findings when he studied the Tzeltal Indians of Oxchuc Mexico. Turner found that the Indians were required to refrain from drinking alcohol when they converted to Protestantism. Consequently, the converts began to save more money. Another benefit noted among the Tzeltal Indians was that "converts who had been taught to repudiate the system of witchcraft were relieved of heavy payments for protection from evil forces" and thus were able to pay off their debts, and improve their socioeconomic standing (Rambo, 1993, p. 148). Turner also reported that "in addition to the effects of conversion in alleviating poverty, disease, and illiteracy, the converts became more involved in their communities. The passivity and hopelessness of the past were replaced by an active and hopeful engagement with their predicament" hence the new converts became their own change agents (as cited in Rambo, 1993, p. 149).

Rambo concluded that conversion is both a process and an event. His systematic stage model of religious conversion should be seen more as multidimensional as opposed to sequential. While the "stages" can be experienced in a sequence, there is often a "spiraling effect" in place as the sequence may be experienced differently by each individual. He sees the process as complicated, both elusive and inclusive, and contends that a "scientific understanding of conversion is merely a human attempt" to comprehend a divine phenomenon (Rambo, 1993, p. 17, 176). Rambo's stages of religious conversion mirrors elements of Rogers' (2003) theory of the Diffusion of Innovations. Richard Bulliet (1979) in his study of conversions to Islam also found that their conversion process mirrored the steps found in Rogers's theory. Chang, Lee and Kim's (2006) study is a more recent study utilizing the Diffusion of Innovations theory. Their characteristic of "perceived needs" and "perceived benefits" are quite similar to Rambo's "quest" and "interaction" stages.

73

Diffusion of Innovations

According to Rogers (2003), diffusion is the process by which an innovation is communicated through certain channels over time among the members of a social system. It is a special type of communication, in that diffusion is concerned with the spread of new ideas. Within this process are four key ingredients which remain standard across cultures, and is usually examined in all diffusion research. The key ingredients are: an innovation, communication channels, time duration, and a social system. Each of these key ingredients will be examined individually.

The Innovation

This includes an idea, practice or object that is perceived as new by an individual or unit of adoption regardless of the lapse of time since its first use or discovery. "If an idea seems new to the individual, it is an innovation" (Rogers, 2003, p. 12). Someone may have known about an innovation for a long time but did not develop a favorable or unfavorable attitude toward it, neither have they adopted or rejected it. The newness, Rogers argued, can be expressed in terms of knowledge, persuasion, or a decision to adopt. Diffusion research centers on the conditions which increase or decrease the likelihood that a new idea, product, or practice will be adopted by members of a given culture (Infante, Rancer & Womack, 1997).

Rogers (2003) characterized the innovation-decision process as an information-seeking and information-processing activity. This is similar to the quest stage of the Rambo (1993) model. During this process individuals are highly motivated to learn more about the new ideas to be able to determine whether the advantages of adopting them out way the disadvantage of rejecting them. The characteristics of the innovation, as perceived by each individual, contribute

74

greatly to the varying degrees of adoption. Rogers (2003) identified five main characteristics of innovations and those innovations perceived as having all of these attributes will be adopted more quickly than those innovations lacking one or more of these characteristics. The five attributes are as follows: The first is *relative advantage*. This is "the degree to which an innovation is perceived as better than the idea it supersedes" (Rogers 2003, p. 15). This degree can be measured in economic terms, social prestige, convenience, and level of satisfaction. It is one of individual perception, and may not be measured in objective terms. The greater the perceived relative advantage of an innovation, the more rapid will be its rate of adoption.

The second attribute is that of *compatibility*. This is the degree to which an innovation is perceived as being consistent with the existing values, past experiences, and needs of the potential adopters. The third factor is that of *complexity*, which is explained as the degree to which an innovation is perceived as difficult to understand and use. New ideas that are straightforward are easier to adopt than those which require the adopter to develop new skills and an increased level of understanding. The fourth characteristic is described as *trial-ability*. This is the degree to which an innovation may be experimented with on a limited basis. An innovation that allows the adopters to test it before embracing it reduces the level of uncertainty and the likelihood of its adoption. The final attribute is that of *observability*. This is the degree to which the results of an innovation are visible to others. "The easier it is for individuals to see the results of an innovation, the more likely they are to adopt" (Rogers, 2003, p. 15-16). Past research indicates that these characteristics are the most essential and are responsible for explaining how individuals adopt new ideas.

Communication Channels

This is the essence of the diffusion process in that information is exchanged among individuals. The means through which this exchange is done is via a channel, be it face to face, or electronically mediated. While mass media channels are usually the most rapid and efficient means of informing an audience of potential adopters about the existence of an innovation, interpersonal channels have proven more effective in persuading an individual to adopt the new idea. In this study, the channel examined was that of the religious radio broadcasts of AWR.

Time

This is the third of four elements in the diffusion process. It measures the period from first knowledge of an innovation through to the decision to adopt or reject the innovation. Rogers (2003) posit that the process includes time spent in each of the following stages: (1) Seeking knowledge about an innovation (2) being persuaded, (3) making a decision to adopt or reject, (4) implementation of the new idea, and finally, (5) confirmation of the decision. Knowledge is gained when an individual (or other decision-making unit) learns of the innovation's existence and gains some understanding of how it works. Persuasion takes place when the individual forms a favorable or unfavorable attitude toward the innovation. Stage three occurs when an individual engages in activities that lead to a choice to adopt or reject, and stage four occurs when the individual puts the innovation into use. When an individual seeks reinforcement of their decision, the final stage, has occurred. If the process is completed in a short period of time, the adopters are considered as innovative.

Rogers (2003) specified five adopter categories: (1) innovators, (2) early adopters, (3) early majority, (4) late majority, and (5) laggards. The *innovators* are those who are adventurous and willing to try new ideas. The second group (the *early adopters)*, are the individuals "to check with before adopting a new idea" (p. 283). The third category is the *early majority*, those who deliberate for sometime before completely adopting a new idea. The *late majority* is the fourth group and is comprised of those who are skeptical, and prefer to wait until most of the other members of their social system have agreed to embrace the new idea. The fifth and final group is that of the *laggards*. These individuals are the last in a social system to adopt an innovation, and are very habitual, preferring to remain committed to their traditional ways.

Many innovations require a lengthy period of many years from the time when they become available to the time when they are widely adopted. The relative speed with which the innovation is adopted by members of the social system is referred to as the rate of adoption. This is usually measured by the number of members of the system who adopt the innovation in a given period of time.

Social System

"Diffusion occurs within a social system. The social structure of the system affects the innovation's diffusion in several ways." (Rogers, 2003, p. 24). The structure of the social system, including its norms, values and the role of the opinion leaders, change agents as well as the consequences of adopting the innovation, all impact the diffusion process. Every social system has both a formal and an informal structure. Individual decisions are affected both by an individual's personality and circumstances, as well as by the nature, influence, and expected consequences imposed by the social system to which they belong. Any kind of social change will face the scrutiny of the social system. Social change is perceived as the process by which alteration occurs in the structure and function of a social

77

system. Rogers (2003) argues that when new ideas are invented, diffused, and adopted or rejected, leading to certain consequences, social change occurs.

Chang, Lee and Kim (2006) created an integrated model of online game adoption by combining the Uses and Gratification Theory (Lazarsfeld & Stanton, 1944) with that of the Diffusion of Innovations. For their study of online game adoption, the original five adopter categories put forth by Rogers were collapsed into four categories, namely: continuers, non-continuers, potentials, and resistors. Their study will now be examined.

Other Diffusion of Innovation Studies

Chang, Lee and Kim (2006), conducted a study on the adoption and continuance of online games among college students in South Korea. They discovered during their literature review that current game studies had not yet considered or examined games as an innovation or new medium. Consequently, their study sought to examine online games from the perspective of the importance of the needs that individuals are attempting to fulfill by using online games. The following definitions of the elements of the diffusion of innovation theory were set forth in the framing of their study.

An integrated model of online game adoption was developed. Users were classified as online game adopters or non-adopters. Adopters were further subdivided into those who continued (continuers), and those who started but discontinued playing online games (non-continuers). The non-adopters included those who have never used online games before, but have expressed intent to try them in the near future (potentials); and the fourth group consisted of those who were reluctant to play online games (resisters).

Four essential constructs were identified with two subcomponents to measure the decision making process of users, as to whether they became adopters

78

or non-adopters. The first was "perceived needs." This construct sought to understand what motivated online game users. Were they playing games online to pass the time, as an attempt to connect with others who shared their passion, or was the appeal the fact that it was an activity they could engage in while in solitude?

The second construct was identified as "inner innovativeness" which was defined in the Rogers study as "the degree to which an individual or other unit of adoption is relatively earlier in adopting an innovation than other members of a social system" (Chang, Lee & Kim, 2006, p. 22). Midgley and Dowling's study (as cited in Chang, Lee & Kim, 2006), defined innovativeness as "the degree to which an individual is receptive to new ideas and makes innovation decisions independently of the communicated experience of others" (p. 236). A theoretical distinction has been made between inherent innovativeness and actualized innovativeness, allowing for the separation of an individual's need for innovativeness and the subsequent action to actualize such a need (Chang, Lee & Kim, 2006).

"Perceived characteristics" was the third construct. This involved the benefits or relative advantage, envisioned by the user or recipient of the new innovation and or idea. Some of the ideas measured by this construct include, how easy or difficult it will be to adopt the innovation; will it be compatible with the old, or will it replace the old. Is the new innovation something that could be experienced on a trial basis? Can others be observed before adoption? Will the innovation be difficult to understand and implement on a long term basis?

The fourth construct was "perceived popularity." How will the user be perceived among family members, friends, peers as well as the society at large? The Diffusion of Innovation theory focuses on the social system and the mass media as sources of information. According to this perspective, an individual receives information regarding an innovation through both mass media and a social

79

system, such as family members, friends, and co-workers. Other studies conducted by Fulk (1993), and Schmitz & Fulk (1991) (as cited in Chang, Lee & Kim, 2006), generally supported the notion that the social system surrounding an individual can affect the individual's innovation adoption. The construct of perceived popularity can therefore be used to measure the influence of social systems.

Several studies in the Diffusion of Innovation have shown that ownership of the new media is a significant predictor for the adoption of the new technology or ideology. Reagan's study (as cited in Chang, Lee & Kim, 2006), found that the adoption of telecommunication technologies was powerfully predicted by the use of other similar technologies and user attitudes toward them. This relationship was also found to encourage the adoption of cable television and computer media. The Diffusion of Innovation theory also assumes that the use of other forms of the mass media will positively affect the inherent innovativeness of individuals, and positively affect the adoption of a new medium because mass media use, leads to the obtaining of information regarding the new medium (Chang, Lee & Kim, 2006).

This study combined the process of religious conversion (Rambo, 1993), the Diffusion of Innovations (Rogers, 2003) and the Chang, Lee and Kim study (2006) on online gaming, to create a theoretical framework for examining AWR's work in Tanzania. The researcher theorized that AWR's broadcasts contributed to the adoption of Adventist religious ideology among members of the Tanzanian population.

CHAPTER 4: METHODOLOGY

This study utilized a qualitative research design in the form of an instrumental case study. According to Creswell (2007), the case study approach allows the researcher to delve deeply into the phenomenon under study within a selected context. It is a "comprehensive research strategy of inquiry" within the qualitative research paradigm which allows for data to be collected from multiple sources such as documents, archival records and physical artifacts (Babbie, 2007). This case study was conducted using a historical systematic methodology. This approach allowed the researcher to utilize several sources of data to "systematically investigate" the work of Adventist World Radio (AWR) in Tanzania (Wimmer & Dominick, 2006).

As a qualitative study, the logic followed was inductive, "from the ground up" which allowed the researcher to sometimes reword research questions during the study to improve the quality of the questions needed to understand the research problem (Creswell, 2007). The findings of this study are therefore "particularistic, descriptive, inductive, and interpretive" (Creswell, 1994; Wimmer & Dominick, 2006). Being particularistic, this case study focused on a specific phenomenon: the process of religious conversion. The results are descriptive in that they provide a description of some of the international religious radio listeners in Tanzania, East-Central Africa, as well as the operations of the international religious broadcaster, AWR. The interpretive approach allowed the researcher to gain and then share a deeper understanding of the phenomenon of religious conversion as a result of international religious broadcasting.

The historical systematic methodology was used to locate and analyze the artifacts identified in the database. The study was designed to describe a 25-year period from 1983-2008, the individuals involved (radio listeners), and the

81

phenomenon (the process of religious conversion), for the purpose of interpreting or evaluating communication and its effects (Reinard, 1998). The term artifact as used in this study represents listener correspondences as well as other archival documents which constitute the data for this study.

Qualitative Research Paradigm

The qualitative research paradigm presupposes the following ontological, epistemological and axiological assumptions. From an ontological perspective, "qualitative researchers embrace the idea of multiple realities. Evidence of multiple realities includes the use of multiple quotes based on the actual words of different individuals and presenting different perspectives from individuals." The epistemological assumption enabled the researcher to "try to get as close as possible to the participants being studied." In this case, handwritten letters found in the archives were highly valued (Creswell, 2007, p. 18). The researcher's religious background was identified in chapter one and the accompanying axiological assumptions were made explicit. Creswell (2007) explained that "in a qualitative study, the inquirers admit the value-laden nature of the study and actively report their values and biases as well as the value-laden nature of information gathered from the field" thus positioning him/herself in the study. This researcher is positioned as both an emic and etic researcher, given her background as a member of the Seventh-day Adventist Church (SDA), the researcher utilizes an emic approach, but she also is an outsider (etic approach), seeing that she does not belong to the geographic region being studied, and neither is she a member of the Adventist World Radio (AWR) network (Niblo & Jackson, 2004).

The qualitative method used was that of the historical systematic

82

methodology. Tosh (2000) argued that "the study of history is a personal matter, in which the activity is generally more valuable than the result...for explanation too can be sought for its own sake" (pp. 29-31). Notwithstanding, a study of the past can yield an interpretation that is "relevant to the present and a basis for formulating decisions about the future" (Tosh, 2000, p. 32). Tosh also believed that "the most revealing source is that which was written with no thought for posterity" (p. 39). Such was the experience of the researcher when reviewing the artifacts found in the archives. Most were not created for use in a study of this nature. With that in mind, let us now examine the historical systematic methodology as used in this study.

Historical Systematic Methodology

The historical systematic methodology, also known as historical methodology, is distinct from other methodological approaches typically utilized in mass media research, but shares with them the requirement to be rigorous and systematic in its protocol. The historical approach allows for the survey of archival data in primary, secondary and tertiary form (Strengholt, 2008). As set forth in Skreslet (2007), there are three requirements in conducting a good historical study. The first is that the written account must be coherent, in the sense that a logical interpretive argument is constructed on the basis of plausible data supported by reputable sources of authority. Second, it should be persuasive, which means putting forward a case that is not just credible but that can move readers to agree with the author's conclusions, even when alternative explanations are given a fair hearing in the presentation. Finally, the most daunting test is that of its significance. This study provides a deeper understanding within the scholarly community, of the phenomenon of religious broadcasting and the process of religious conversion, through the examination of documents that reveal how one international religious broadcaster carried out its stated mission.

Howell and Prevenier (2001) agreed that sources are artifacts that have been left by the past. A source provides evidence about the existence of an event. The significance of the event however greatly depends on what happened before and after the event. Sources need to be identified and viewed in a historical context, not as isolated pieces of information. Once sources are contextualized and authenticated, then the researcher can embark on a historical interpretation of the data often found in archives. Archives are central locations for sources of information; but even when an archive exists it is not always available to scholars. Private archives are technically closed and can be consulted only with the permission of the owner. Even public archives are often restricted. According to mutually agreed upon international conventions, access to documents less than 30 years old can be denied to safeguard the protection of those involved, or to avoid embarrassment based on the information revealed (Howell & Prevenier, 2001).

Once the sources have been procured, the next step is that of authenticating each source. This is done by critically examining the origins of the source. Howell and Prevenier (2001) provide seven points of critical textual analysis which they also describe as source criticism. The first is the "genealogy of the document." In validating its genealogy, the researcher must determine if the document is an original, a copy of the original, or a copy of a copy. A second examination point is described as "the genesis of the document" that is, when and where it was composed, and by whom? The third point of examination is that of its "authorial authority," meaning with what authority does the source speak? Was the author an eye witness to the events he or she describes, or did he or she participate in the design of the system? The fourth point is the "originality of the document." This

84

questions whether this is the first instance of such a principle or event in the culture being studied; as well as where and in what social setting the document was produced.

"Interpretation of the document" is the fifth point of consideration. This involves deciphering the intended meaning of the source and the purpose for which it was produced. The sixth step involves determining the "competency of the observer." At this juncture, the researcher asks: what was the psychological state of the author of the source? Was he or she satisfied with life, or bitter about his or her circumstances? Are there events, or parts of the story that he or she may have been likely to ignore? Under what outside influences was the source constructed? Was there censorship or scrutiny? The seventh and final point of source authentication is that of the "trustworthiness of the observer." Are there factors mitigating against the willingness of the observer to tell what he considers to be the truth? (Howell & Prevenier, 2001). Once the sources have been identified and validated, then the researcher can embark on a historical interpretation of the facts. A historical interpretation is an argument about the event which is formulated after a careful examination of available sources. This is accomplished by doing a source comparison, which can be completed in the following seven steps.

(1) If the sources all agree about an event, historians can consider the event proven.

(2) All the documents must pass the test of critical analysis.

(3) Sources can be confirmed by reference to outside authorities in at least some of its parts, if not its entirety.

(4) When two sources disagree, the historian will prefer the source with the most "authority," that is, the source created by the expert or the eyewitness.

(5) Eye witness accounts are to be preferred at all times.

(6) If two independently created sources agree on a matter, the reliability of each is measurably enhanced.

(7) When two sources disagree and there is no other means of evaluation, then historians take the source which seems to accord best with common sense (Howell & Prevenier, 2001).

Despite all the procedures available to authenticate a source, Howell and Prevenier (2001) caution that pure objectivity is an unattainable goal. Researchers are admonished to analyze and read documents meticulously, while acknowledging their limitations. Sources can only be interpreted from the standpoint of the researcher's position. The researcher's beliefs will shape his or her interpretation of the events and sources examined. The goal of the researcher should be that of helping others to see events from their point of view by producing useful knowledge about the past, or at least about the past to which the researcher had a privileged access. Historical methodology is a qualitative form of research which is also systematic and rigorous. It draws conclusions and presents new explanations about past communication events based on an inductive review of archival material.

The following segment outlines the research design which guided the study. The research design includes "the entire process of research from conceptualizing a problem to writing research questions, and on to data collection, analysis, interpretation, and report writing" (Creswell, 2007, p. 5). Chapters one and two outlined the conceptualization of the research problem and the actual questions examined. The focus of this upcoming section therefore will be that of explaining how the data was collected, analyzed and interpreted.

Research Design

The data gathered for this study were "a wide spectrum of evidence" (Wimmer & Dominick, 2006, p. 137). The data set included minutes, memos, contracts, internal documents, studio reports and other historical records such as personal listener correspondences sent to the AWR network from members of the listening audience. In addition to these primary sources, secondary sources were also consulted. These included newsletters, annual reports, organizational yearbooks, the network's website, magazines, promotional DVDs, and other publications of the organization. These artifacts, collected through the years directly from listeners, program partners, as well as studio managers abroad, have been archived at the world head quarters of the Seventh-day Adventist (SDA) church and can be accessed through the Office of Archives and Statistics in Silver Spring, MD, or directly from the AWR office.

Data Collection

Prior to each visit to the archives, an appointment was made with an associate of the Office of Archives and Statistics. For each appointment, security clearance had to be obtained before gaining access to the offices within the building. Once the check-in process was complete, the archive associate would then provide a printed copy of the Records Center File Report from which the researcher would request the files needed. The Records Center File Report contained a description of each department within the SDA organization. Other file identification markers included a record identification label, a record number, accession number, accession date, creation date, box number, and a user box number. The system allowed for a fairly accurate process of retrieving archival documents by department (example, AWR; East-Central Africa Division); by label (example, name of country-Tanzania); as well as by date and location within the archive.

Some of the listener mails which served as primary sources for the study were in their original form, still bearing the postage stamps of their country of origin. They also bore an organizational stamp which indicated when they were received at the radio station, and what action was taken. Some of the letters appeared quite frail; therefore, a significant amount of time was needed on site to review those artifacts and to determine which ones fell within the geographic and time limitations established for the study. Photocopies were made of documents that could be duplicated; for those too frail for duplication, notes were recorded in a research journal. Within the Office of Archives and Statistics, there was a laser photocopier, and copies were made at the cost of eight cents per page.

Electronic files were also obtained directly from the AWR president. Based on the country of focus, most of the electronic files were of a "no restrictions" classification which allowed for them to be used publicly without needing to conceal the source. For personal listener correspondences however, confidentiality measures have been put in place, and their identities are not revealed. The duration of this project encompassed three years.

Challenges

The following challenges were foreseen and accommodations were made in the execution of this research design. Firstly, in acquiring needed materials and information, multiple requests were made before some of the resources were obtained. Secondly, given that the files were not compiled with this study in mind, there were instances in which essential details were missing such as the date, author, or source credentials of the artifact. The AWR letters & stories (April 23, 2004) for example, included first quarter reports from "Sam." This primary source did not reveal who Sam was. Upon further exploration of secondary and tertiary sources, it was discovered that Sam was the AWR-Africa region director (Freesland, 2005). Triangulation was therefore implemented by reviewing other artifacts to determine the original source or intended recipients based on job titles, social setting, personnel assignments, as well as the historical chronology of a given incident or ongoing events.

The researcher recognized that the listener correspondences and other archival documents available for examination, constituted a non-probability sample of the actual AWR operations and listener feedback from Tanzania. Consequently the researcher recognized the lack of control over which listener correspondences, or archival documents were available and was unable to "go back in time" to fill in the missing pieces. The researcher therefore relied on available artifacts which may impact the internal and external validity of the study. To the extent possible, face and content validity was however sought and achieved. The researcher recognized her personal values and their influence on the interpretations nonetheless this study provides explanations that go beyond common sense knowledge through the systematic rigor of historical research.

Data Analysis Techniques

Data analysis entailed the creation of a database and sub-databases for comparative assessment. This allowed the researcher to methodically review areas of incongruence within the data gathered from different sources. The subsets allowed the researcher to scan data for each variable within the study, and be able to compare and contrast findings more readily. Some of the categories included gender, geographic region, reason for corresponding, source of the information and the date the artifact was created or reported to AWR. Other considerations included the population of each SDA conference in Tanzania, the number of churches and members, local church activities, educational, medical, and other developmental church sponsored agencies and institutions, as well as other media initiatives being employed by the SDA church within the same area.

Within the media initiatives category, consideration was given to literature evangelism, satellite evangelism and Bible correspondence courses. Listener mails received from each Tanzanian SDA conference, the date of each correspondence, similarities in letter content, the number of multiple correspondences from the same source, the type of information being provided and or requested, and how the network addressed each correspondence, were also examined. The correspondences were analyzed according to Rambo's (1993) process of religious conversion and key concepts of the Diffusion of Innovation theory (Rogers, 2003).

While the data for each category were being compiled, the researcher engaged in the process of verification, validation and interpretation of the documents gathered before formulating the qualitative narrative (Creswell, 2007). As explained by Howell and Prevenier (2001), a historical interpretation needs to be provided in the form of an argument which is formulated after a careful examination of available sources. This was accomplished by doing a source comparison as outlined earlier in this study.

Table 1 provides a summary of the artifacts which were integral to this study.

Table 1: Summary of Database

(Based on Howell & Prevenier's (2001) points of critical textual analysis)

1	2	3	4	5	6
Type of Artifacts	**Number of Artifacts**	**Genealogy**	**Historical Period**	**Source Authority**	**Trustworthiness**
Contracts	1		1983		
Memos/Reports/ Committee Minutes	13	Copies of original documents	1984-2003	Gatekeepers & Eyewitnesses	Sources named can be verified by the SDA Office of Archives & Statistics
Compilations of Listener responses/ letters & Stories	56		1988-2009		
Magazines/ Newsletters/ Newspaper Articles	20		1967-2005		
Brochures & Other Promotional Materials	4		1994-2001		
Miscellaneous: Studio Directories	2		1999; 2009		
Total/Range	**96**		**1967-2009**		

The first category in Table 1 deals with the type of documents found in the database. Column two sums the number of artifacts used within each category. Column three identifies each document in the researcher's possession as a copy of original documents because originals could not be taken from the archives.

Column four shows the dates associated with each category of documents with the magazine and newspaper articles being the widest ranging in dates. Column five summarizes the source in two categories: gatekeepers and eyewitnesses with the former referring to all source that generated artifacts, except for the actual listeners. The published database includes measures to safeguard the privacy of each listener correspondent. The AWR personnel submitting the report is identified, but the actual listeners' identification are not revealed. In the findings chapter, listeners are referred to as coded, example. *Listener A1* based on the question the information is used to answer. The locations of listeners are reported according to the SDA Conferences in the region, as opposed to the listeners' exact addresses. The researcher recognized that revealing personal information without prior consent from the listeners would be unethical and thus refrained from doing so. Each document analyzed was evaluated according to the Howell and Prevenier (2001) points of critical analysis, and yielded the following results.

Source Criticism

Also known as a critical textual analysis, source criticism is a process undertaken by the researcher to authenticate the artifacts being used in the study. Howell and Prevenier (2001) were very instrumental in outlining the necessary steps. The first step in authenticating sources comes in the form of examining the "genealogy of the documents." Most of the documents used in this study were acquired in one of four ways: (1) They were personally handled and or photocopied in the SDA Office of Archives and Statistics, (2) they were received via email from AWR personnel; (3) They were transferred directly from the AWR President's database to the researchers external hard drive; and (4) they were downloaded from the SDA online Archives. The researcher's personal involvement with each artifact helped to ensure its genealogy as they were an original, a copy of the original, or a copy of a copy. A second examination point was "the genesis of the document." The researcher was able to determine this by checking for a date, stamp, name, job title, or address which would indicate where the document originated and who was its intended recipient. The researcher was successful in determining this for all except one entry in the database for which no name or date was provided. The name of the publication and its sponsor were the only identifying markers for that entry.

Examining the "authority of the source" was the third point of examination. Eighty percent of the sources used were created by reporters, gate-keepers, other AWR personnel, while only 20 % were derived directly from listeners. Some of the gatekeeper reports were compilations of listener mails but they were in excerpt form. Most of the authors were therefore participants in the "the design of the system" even though they may not have been eye-witnesses to the stories they reported. Deciphering the intended meaning of the document was not always clear cut; not because the content was complicated, but because the interpretation was by nature subjective, and shaped by the researcher's knowledge and beliefs. Most of the reports were written to provide status updates on ongoing projects, breaking news, and note worthy listener interactions. A favorably judgment was also made by the researcher on the part of the "competency of the observer" because there were no glaring indicators of the sources experiencing any psychological imbalance, bitterness or dissatisfaction with life in general. On the contrary, the reports were usually up-beat and optimistic about what God had done, or was expected to do.

Having completed the identification and validation of the sources, the researcher is now free to embark upon a historical interpretation of the facts. This could only be done after a careful examination of the available sources. The authentification process allowed the researcher to draw conclusions and explanations about past communication events based on an inductive review of archival material.

CHAPTER 5: FINDINGS, INTERPRETATION AND DISCUSSION

This study was conducted using a historical systematic methodology to gather and analyze artifacts pertaining to Adventist World Radio's (AWR) operations in Tanzania, East Central Africa. The study was limited to a 25-year period from 1983-2008, which marks the first 25 years of AWR-Africa's operations. The archival materials analyzed reveal that the SDA Church has a global mission and the organization is making strides in its fulfillment. Of the six conferences and field within the Tanzania Union Mission (TUM), the South Nyanza Conference (SNC) had the highest proportion of SDA Churches, but it was the Mara Conference (MC) which had the lowest SDA member to population ratio. The East Tanzania Conference (ETC), home to the AWR studio, had the highest percentage of listener mail, but still remains one of the largest mission fields for the SDA Church as the SDA member to population ratio is 1:202, in comparison to the Mara Conference which has a ratio of 1:19. The ETC's ratio serves as a constant reminder that conversion is a process which occurs through channels and advocates in a social system, over time.

The Southern Highlands Conference (SHC) also remains an area of great need where the SDA Church's mission activities are concerned. There are currently approximately 35 thousand SDA members in the SHC, in a population of six million. This equates to a member to population ratio of 1:176. This also places the SHC in the top priority category for international evangelistic outreach as the number of local SDA members within the region is comparatively low. There are signs, however, of AWR's impact as the second highest number of listener correspondences were received from this region. West Tanzania remains a mission field with its 42 thousand SDA members in a population of 8.5 million, a ratio of

95

1:203. A very small percentage of listener correspondences were obtained from this region. Figure 4 presents a comparative view of the number of listener correspondences analyzed for this study, per TUM conference/field.

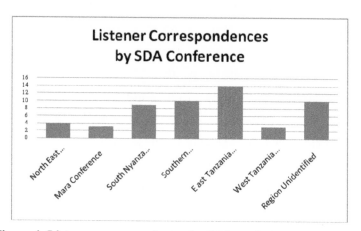

Figure 4: Listener correspondences by SDA conference

The SDA Church is one worldwide Church and resources are harnessed and distributed according to the areas of greatest need. The remainder of this chapter presents the research findings according to the questions posed, and a discussion of the findings will follow according to the theoretical framework used to guide the study.

Research Question

The overarching question which guided the study was:

To what extent has Adventist World Radio succeeded in fulfilling the Seventh-day Adventist Church's mission within the Tanzania Union Mission of Seventh-day Adventists?

The SDA Church's mission is far from complete within the regions of the TUM. The country's population is estimated at 45 million while the SDA membership in the TUM is approximately 450 thousand. This yields an SDA member to population ratio of 1:97. The AWR broadcasts can be heard throughout the TUM conferences. The conference in which the AWR studio is located generated most of the listener correspondences analyzed however the proportion of SDA members in comparison to the size of the population in this region remains rather low. Findings show that the Mara Conference has the lowest ratio while the West Tanzania Field has the highest member to population ratio. Figure 5 shows a comparison of SDA membership to the population of each regional conference/ field. The figure was created by the researcher based on the statistical information obtained from the SDA Yearbook (2011).

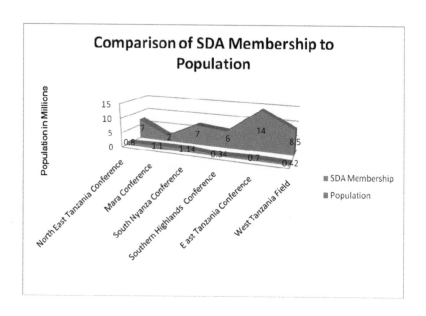

Figure 5: Comparison of SDA membership to population

As the findings for the remaining questions show, there are several factors which influence how the SDA Church develops its evangelistic strategies, and the membership to population ratio is but one of them. The TUM is one of seven unions within the East-Central Africa Division and occupies the third structural level from the General Conference of Seventh-day Adventists. Some of the mission goals and strategies are created at the GC level, while others are developed at the Division and Union levels so that they are specific to the location regions in which they will be carried out. The findings reveal that it is too early to declare the mission accomplished; hence, the success attained is only partial. What is clear however is that the SDA Church is advancing on multiple fronts and using various avenues to spread the Christian message. These avenues include radio broadcasts, satellite evangelism, literature evangelism, education and medical services, among others.

The SDA Church's mission is based on the verses of scripture outlined in the gospel of Matthew: 28:18-20 and placed in the context of the three angels messages of Revelation 14: 6-12. The mission statement can be divided into four facets: (1) Proclaiming the Christian message to all nations, kindred, tongue and people, (2) Leading them to accept Jesus and (3) Uniting with His church, while (4) Nurturing them in preparation for His soon return (SDA Yearbook, 2011). One measure of success can be seen when church members partner with the radio network in proclaiming the gospel message (J. Abrahams, listener responses, July 23, 2004). This Abrahams sees as an extension of AWR's reach.

An example of church members in such a partnership can be derived from listener responses (J. Abrahams, July 23, 2004) in which one writer expressed his appreciation for the Bible themes presented in the radio programs. *Listener A1* stated that two weeks in advance of the radio programs, he took a leadership role at his church in preparing listeners for the broadcasts. He was now pleased to report that 21 students were identified, with 7 enrolling in the Bible Correspondence School for further studies. One of his listeners even requested that the evangelistic programs be replayed on air at least once every quarter. He concluded his report by stating that in Iringa (Southern Highlands Conference/ SHC), there were many listeners of AWR. Another SHC listener, *Listener A2*, commended the network for making his job easier. He indicated that the network's presentations of difficult Bible passages were helping him to better present the SDA message to his neighbors, friends and relatives. He saw the network's mission as that of preaching the word of God both to believers and non-believers.

Another measure of success is that of being able to broadcast the AWR programs in local languages. *Listener A3* wrote: "I must congratulate leaders and ministers in AWR Maasai service who strive to serve and speak this language in a very perfect way" (L. Kibasisi, AWR letters & stories, September 27, 2006). It was interesting to note that the listener perceived the network's efforts as that of "striving to serve and speak" which would suggest that there may be room for improvement. In the church's efforts to proclaim the Christian message to all nations, kindred, tongue and people, as much as possible, native speakers are used in the preparation and presentation of broadcasts.

The local producer of the AWR Maasai language programs seized an invitation to attend a gathering of Maasai people on the occasion of the retirement of the *Morans* and the passing of the tribal responsibilities to the younger age-group known as the *Irkorinaga* (AWR letters & stories, September 27, 2006). The AWR Maasai language program producer was one of several pastors invited to speak at the event, and he in turn invited the Women's Ministries Director of the Eastern Tanzania Conference to attend. The Director was tasked to speak on the subject of women circumcision/ Female Genital Mutilation (FGM). The producer was pleased to report that both of their presentations were well received and that just being invited to attend the event was a breakthrough as in the past only ritual leaders were asked to participate.

"Nurturing them in preparation for His soon return" is the fourth and final facet of the SDA church's mission statement. Support for that undertaking, can be seen in several listener correspondences which indicated that the programs have strengthened them, and that they have been richly blessed by the teachings. *Listener A4*, considered the radio host as "a hero in the Lord's work" while *Listener A5* admitted that he/she "was a backslider, but through the Adventist radio I am now strengthened" (L. Kibasisi, AWR letters & stories, September 27, 2006). These samples of listener correspondences indicate a partnership between the AWR network, local SDA members and radio listeners. The following excerpts

100

and paraphrases serve to present the varied voices of other AWR listeners as they relate to the more specific research questions posed for this study.

Research Question # 1a

What factors contribute to the SDA church's engagement in the use of Religious radio broadcasts to fulfill their stated global mission within the Tanzania Union Mission?

The findings reveal at least four factors contributing to the SDA Church's use of radio to fulfill the stated mission. The first factor presented was that of the degree of freedom prevalent in the country, (2) the number of SDA members within the population, (3) the ability of the local church organization to fund its own initiatives, and (4) the availability of personnel to follow-up on the contacts initiated by AWR. These factors were identified upon careful review of division reports, websites, reports published from missionaries in the field, and personal correspondences. The findings help us to understand why AWR would choose to broadcast in Tanzania. There is relative freedom of the press, there is a small SDA membership within the country's population, and based on the nation's economy, the local conferences may not be able to entirely fund all the outreach initiatives planned for the area, hence the opportunity to partner with the AWR network to do the follow-up visits requested by AWR listeners.

The findings also reveal that the SDA Church is very systematic in its planning and coordination of initiatives to fulfill its mission. The organizational structure of the world church is as such that areas of the world that have a large percentage of the population classified as "unreached" will receive international assistance in their evangelism efforts. Entities such as AWR are not limited to any local division or union; hence they are free to operate according to the areas determined by the General Conference (GC) as having the greatest need. Now let us examine each factor more closely.

According to Dr. Schoun, former president of AWR, the network has established criteria which are used to determine broadcast priorities. The first criterion identified by AWR is that of the "Freedom Limitation Factor" (FLF). This is decided by examining the annual reports of media entities such as *Freedom House*, *Reporters without Borders* and other organizations which study the changing field of press freedoms around the world. Countries with restrictions on their freedom will have a higher priority ranking for AWR to broadcast there. A second determinant is the "Global Mission Challenge Factor" (GMCF). This is a formula devised by the Adventist Mission Department of the world church which reflects the ratio of Adventist membership to the population, taking into consideration the level of any representation of Christianity there as well. The fewer Christians (or Adventists) in relationship to the population, the higher priority it is for AWR. The formula can be computed based on the population of each country in thousands, divided by the SDA church membership, multiplied by the country population in thousands again. This is then converted to a scale of 100-500 points, with 500 being the area of greatest need (B. Schoun, personal communication, April 14, 2000).

Another factor contributing to the decision of whether to prepare broadcasts for a particular region is based on the local church's financial need. Areas where the SDA church receives a low proportion of tithes and offerings, and where the economy is very poor, results in that area having a higher priority in the international broadcaster's budget and operations. The formula used here is the total tithe reported for the country, divided by the population, multiplied by the Gross Domestic Product (GDP), according to purchasing power. Some countries

102

have a big mission, but very limited resources to accomplish it. Therefore the poorer the country, the higher priority it is for AWR. The fourth factor is that of media availability. To determine this factor, the network asks, "Do the people in this country have access to any other Adventist media broadcasts?" If there is little or no access to other broadcast media, then the region is a high priority for AWR (B. Schoun, personal communication, April 14, 2010).

Several GC Departments play a part in strategic planning for global missions. The formula used by AWR was created by the Adventist Mission Department, and from time to time the AWR Board meets to review its project reports and to strategize for the years ahead based on demographic changes within the SDA Church membership. During a planning session, the results of the data for each factor were scaled with the highest number of points reflective of the most severe area of need. Other factors also come into play, such as "the possibility to create a project in the area, the willingness of the local church officials to be involved, and other practical factors" (B. Schoun, personal communication, April 14, 2010). In the case of Eastern Africa, there is a large SDA church membership (the second largest of the 13 SDA world divisions), but their economic situation is such that they are still classified as needing international assistance.

Research Question # 1b

How has AWR's expansion of broadcast languages to include Maasai language programs, contributed to the growing number of Adventist members within the Tanzania Union Mission?

Since the inception of Maasai language programs in 2001, the numbers of SDAs among the Maasai people have grown exponentially. It is likely that this trend will continue to increase as the SDA Church continues to take advantage of all the available means of spreading the gospel message. Proclaiming the Christian message to all nations, kindred, tongue and people is a part of the Church's mandate and expanding the number of broadcast languages used by AWR is seen as a means of carrying out that mandate.

It was during a special Maasai camp meeting held at Misima Handeni in 1999 that Pastor Geoffrey Mbwana recommended that the Maasai language become one of the languages broadcasted from AWR's studio in Tanzania. Two years later, in April 2001, the Maasai language program was launched at the Morogoro studio and two pastors fluent in the Maasai language, joined the AWR staff. The first Maasai language program went on the air October 28, 2001(L. Kibasisi, AWR letters & stories, December 12, 2005). By the end of 2004, they had produced 343 programs. Kibasisi, producer of the Maasai language programs, noted that due to illiteracy and the environment, there were few responses by mail and emails. He also noted that because the Maasai programs were also being aired in Kenya, some of the listener correspondences were sent to the Nairobi studio and the delay in responding to the letters may have discouraged some listeners from attempting further correspondences.

Despite the challenges, several mass baptisms were reported as direct outcomes of the radio broadcasts. This resulted in more international support being given to assist the Maasai with the acquisition of radios. The results are encouraging, but the Maasai language producer cautioned that there was a lot more follow-up work to be done, than there were workers to do it. Kibasisi (AWR letters & stories, December 12, 2005) cited various oral responses he received from SDA church members who informed him personally, of the program's effectiveness. Kibasisi also reported that he received a message from some lay workers in Kenya who stated that it was becoming a challenge for them to keep up with the baptismal

104

requests. He cited a communication he received from Celeste Lee in November 2005 which reported that there were many converts waiting to be baptized and they had been waiting for a long time. Kibasisi ended this segment of his report by saying: "The harvest is great, but the laborers are few" (L. Kibasisi, AWR letters & stories, December 12, 2005).

Kibasisi's annual report (2005) also cited several mass baptisms, which were linked directly to AWR's programs. He noted the rapid expansion of the SDA church in both Kenya and Tanzania in support of his arguments, noting that the Maasai churches had expanded to more than 10,000 people, all newly converted. Another vivid example of church growth as a result of the Maasai language programs is that of the one-day baptism of 66 Maasai people in the Mballa village, Bagamoyo district, on the Dar-es-Salaam Chalinze Highway. Prior to that event, there were several smaller baptisms as a result of evangelistic activities conducted by youth groups affiliated with the Manzese SDA church (East Tanzania Conference). On November 26, 2005, 38 people were baptized, followed by another 72 being baptized just one week later. Kibasisi posited that AWR was an "air force" which broke down the barriers and made it easier for the local congregations to do the follow-up. He stated, "Many are already touched, they just try to look where to surrender." His report cautioned however, that if the church delayed its follow-up efforts, the new converts may be forced to join other denominations (L. Kibasisi, AWR letters & stories, December 12, 2005). In Mballa, the church membership was growing so rapidly that the conference leaders were contemplating launching Maasai district churches.

Listener B1 residing and working among the Maasai people of the Bagamoyo district, Pwani Province, constantly used the Maasai service of AWR as a medium for evangelism. She opened her horned loud speakers connected to her radio and attracted large numbers of Maasai listeners daily. She was very happy about the practice because it proved effective. *Listener B1* described herself as a "self-supporting evangelist" for the Maasai people, since an early age. She has created several worship groups and companies as a result of her house to house visits and her ministry as a choir teacher (L. Kibasisi, AWR letters & stories, December 13, 2004).

Another report from the church at Mungeta cited the use of the AWR Maasai programs to evangelize more than 200 Maasai people in a nearby community. In 2005, there were two evangelistic campaigns held via the AWR broadcasts: one was held for three weeks in April-May, 2005 and the other in October-November, 2005. As a result, the AWR Maasai language producer said there were several phone calls received from listeners indicating a positive impact, and individuals were being prepared for baptism. It was also reported that some Pentecostal Churches were capitalizing on the AWR programs and doing the in-person follow-ups. Kibasisi said he had to visit the area to confirm that the radio message was affiliated with the SDA church. Kibasisi ended this segment of his report by stating: "Though we don't know the exact number of converts at length the church will realize the harvest of Maasai converts" (L. Kibasisi, AWR letters & stories, December 13, 2004).

According to an article published in the *Transmissions* newsletter (Freesland, 2005, autumn), two donors were identified who were committed to partnering with AWR to provide 250 shortwave radios to the Maasai people. Their monetary contributions also included funding for an entire year of broadcasts in the Maasai language. The AWR archives included a letter of appreciation from the Maasai language program producer. In his letter dated April 20, 2005, Kibasisi recounted the oral history of the Maasai, and described them as a Nilo-Hamitic race who was once aggressive, proud cattle herders, in need of nothing until diseases began to subdue their cattle and man-power. Now they were open to

106

receiving the word of God. He concluded his letter by saying he believed the work the SDA church is doing among the Maasai will bring fruits and the donors would not regret the gifts they gave (L. Kibasisi, AWR letters & stories, April 20, 2005).

A complementary initiative was undertaken to establish listening stations across the Maasai region. These are established with a solar powered radio and a megaphone placed in strategic locations where local SDA church members trained in lay evangelism, can do the follow-up. In the North East Tanzania Conference (NETC), where there is a large Maasai population, 86 Maasai listener stations were established. In the Eastern Tanzania conference (ETC), 80 Maasai listener stations were established. South Nyanza Conference (SNC) followed with 18 established listener stations, 16 in the South West Tanzania Field (SWTF), while the Mara Conference, which has a smaller Maasai population on the side of the Serengeti, received 10 radios to be situated as listener stations (L. Kibasisi, AWR letters & stories, March 2, 2007).

By June 19, 2008, positive stories were emerging from the Maasai listener stations established in 2007. In Kiteto (Ndotoi, Laiseli), where a two-week gospel campaign was conducted, 11 people were baptized, including three *Bomas* (Maasai compounds/ villages). Several requests were made from neighboring villages for similar campaigns to be conducted. The campaign consisted of daytime as well as nighttime programs. A projector was used to show Maasai choirs in VCD and DVD, Jesus films in the Maasai language, along with other prerecorded programs. The Maasai radio producer also gave live presentations. He reported that they had few listeners by day but approximately 1,000 by night. While Kibasisi was pleased to report the heuristic nature of the listener stations that had been established, he was also concerned that he could experience burn out if more workers were not hired as he was the only one responsible for producing, presenting and also going out for field recordings.

The findings have shown that the Maasai language programs have resulted in numerous baptisms among the Maasai people, along with the establishment of several listener stations which expands AWR's reach. Now that we have examined how the SDA Church goes about its mission, and the impact of the Maasai language broadcasts, let us turn our attention to the actual programs that listeners showed a preference for.

Research Question # 1c

Which AWR programs have listeners indicated a preference for by specifically identifying them in their correspondences?

AWR listeners have been very expressive about their favorite programs. The correspondences reviewed indicate that the programs which focused on Marriage and Family Life had a committed listener base that engaged in dialog with the radio network. Studies related to radio and entertainment-education programs (as presented in the review of literature), also featured vibrant dialog between radio stations and listeners on topics related to marriage and family life. Some of the other programs identified by name include *Siri za Ushindi* (Secrets of Success), *Sera za Ndoa* (Marriage Principles; as citied by *Listener C2*), and the *Youth and Life* (as cited by *Listener C3*). *Listener C1* indicated in his/her correspondence that s/he started listening to AWR in March 2003 with a group of other listeners. They were most impressed with the program on marriage by Pr. Onyango. After *Listener C1* received his/her own radio, s/he developed a liking for other AWR programs as well (S. Misiani, AWR letters & stories, April 23, 2004).

Listener C4 was a Seventh-day Adventist who listened to the network daily. She loved the music and programs that provide encouragement. In her correspondence, she identified the programs for each day and indicated how they have been a blessing to her. She noted: Sundays: Adventures; Mondays: Youth and Life (also cited by *Listener C3*; and *Listener C4*); Tuesdays: Marriage (also cited by *Listener C1* and *Listener C4*); Wednesdays: Success Secrets; Thursdays: Health Education; Fridays: Fundamental Teachings.

Listener C5 liked the *Voice of Prophecy* Bible program, especially the lesson on trust for which he identified a specific date (aired November 26, 1997). This listener, a teenage male, wrote his letter the day after the program aired and noted how enlightening the presentation was on "how pornography and fantasy go together." He noted that he himself faced many temptations and only God is perfect. He thanked the network for airing such good teachings and encouraged them to keep the program on the air (Handwritten letter, November 27, 1997).

Listener C6 wrote to congratulate the network for the work they were doing and was particularly impressed with a program on "speaking in tongues." S/he indicated that they called all their friends and encouraged them to tune in. The listener (writing on behalf of a group), noted that they were enjoying the programs related to the yearlong theme of evangelism, and concluded that the program on speaking in tongues was so well done that they felt much love for the speaker even though they didn't know him personally. The listener expressed the hope that they shall meet "in the heavenly paradise" (J. Abrahams, listener responses, July 23, 2004). "Fundamental teachings" was identified by *Listener C7* as the program that had been enriching from the beginning. The listener noted that their non-Adventist visitors are enjoying it very much as well. *Listener C8* and her family liked *Sera za Ndoa* by Pr. Njema. *Listener C8* said that her family was grateful for the programs

109

and they were praying that the presenter would not become tired of working for the Lord.

As was evidenced by these correspondences, the AWR network has regular listeners who tune in to their favorite broadcasts weekly. Some were able to explain how many years they've been listening, and which programs were rich blessings to them. Other correspondents had other reasons for communicating with the network. A portion of these correspondences will now be shared.

Research Question # 1d

What reasons did AWR listeners in Tanzania express for corresponding with the AWR network?

Four main reasons were identified among the listeners for corresponding with the AWR network. The most frequent was that of showing appreciation. Other reasons included seeking spiritual advice, requesting Bible study guides, and prayer requests. *Listener D1* resided in the coastal region and began his/her correspondence as follows: "I have seen it fit to write you and congratulate you for the good work you are doing at AWR." The listener then went on to explain that as a result of being blessed by the programs, they decided to help others to receive a blessing too. The listener was able to do so by connecting a loud speaker to their small radio, thereby broadcasting to the entire village. The listener then concluded his/her correspondence by saying the entire village was being richly blessed as they were learning the word of God through AWR. *Listener D2* explained in his/her correspondence that s/he first started listening to AWR one day while visiting his/her neighbor. The listener said that the teachings brought them so much joy that they had to write to the network to "congratulate [them] for the good work [they] were doing" (J. Abrahams, listener responses, July 23, 2004). This

110

correspondence included the wish that God would add more blessings on the network.

Seeking spiritual advice encapsulates the second category of correspondences. *Listener D3* sought advice on marital issues and also indicated how much the programs were a blessing to him/her. The listener explained that s/he was also a "promoter of AWR." Another listener, *Listener D4,* was writing to acknowledge that they did receive the spiritual advice given to them, and by the grace of God they would be applying the advice received. The correspondence did not include the specifics of the initial request. *Listener D5* described him/herself as a "student preacher" who was enjoying the sermons and seeking advice on how s/he could become a better preacher. *Listener D5's* correspondence included several other elements. She/he was "involved in full time evangelism among children, young people and families" and his/her prayer request was for a fruitful ministry which would include conducting evangelistic meetings. The listener also used the same correspondence to request copies of the *Light of the World* Bible Study Guides. *Listener D6* was also requesting Bible Study Guides. In his/her correspondence, the listener stated, "people are so much interested with your programs and here I have 35 fellows who listen to your aired programs. Therefore kindly send us more of Bible lessons that we may learn more."

Prayer requests were the fourth main category of correspondences. *Listener D7* explained that they needed the Lord's plan to be evident in their life, and so they were requesting prayers so that "the power of darkness would be defeated." Other correspondences fell in multiple categories, while some were unique. One listener explained that he/she was a student and did not own a radio; neither could they afford to buy one. Their ability to listen was dependent on whether there was a radio nearby. Their appeal was for the network to send them the names and addresses of network personnel that they could correspond with to receive

111

information about the topics covered in the programs. *Listener D8* identified other listeners in Japan by name, as they recall hearing the Asian listener's correspondence being read on the radio. The listener, residing in the Mara Conference, requested that the network sends the contact information for some of the listeners in Japan so that they could correspond with each other and exchange views. This handwritten letter was mailed from Tanzania to the AWR office in England in 1990, several years before the AWR studio opened in Tanzania. Other listeners requested that the network increase the airtime for the programs. *Listener D9* in the Mara Conference stated that he was listening daily with many other brothers, and they appreciated what the network was doing; their only request was for more airtime.

The reasons given therefore for corresponding with the network included: submitting prayer requests, seeking spiritual advice, requesting Bible Study Guides, and simply expressing their delight in the programs, and their best wishes for more uplifting broadcasts. Most of the listener correspondences analyzed originated in the East Tanzania Conference, followed by the South West and South Nyanza Conferences. An equally significant proportion of the original cities/ towns however were undetermined. Even so, it was usually clear why the listener was corresponding with the network. The final category of correspondences to be addressed, is that of the potential converts; those who have expressed their decision to join the Adventist Church. Our final research question addresses this group of correspondences and archival documents.

Research Question # 1e

In what ways have listeners within Tanzania, conveyed to the network an interest in learning more about Adventism?

Three communication channels were widely used by listeners who expressed an interest in Adventism. Some wrote directly to the network using regular mail, and more recently, email. Others communicated via telephone, while the majority of the reports that could be classified as conversion stories, were told through a face to face encounter with a third party who reported to the AWR network on the listeners' behalf. The importance of person to person contact was underscored throughout the communications related to this question. Studio reports told of requests received from the field from listening groups who were waiting to see a representative from the SDA Church before making a full commitment to an organization they had only come to know via the radio. Others told of face to face reports from local pastors who felt overwhelmed by the number of baptism requests, knowing that they must first spend time examining the candidates' knowledge and commitment to Adventism before actually baptizing them. Before addressing the face to face requests, let me present those interests conveyed via mail.

In the *Second Quarter Report* (July 23, 2004), *Listener E1* indicated in their correspondence that s/he was a member of another religious faith, "but through your teachings I have joined your church." *Listener E2* states that s/he was a Roman Catholic believer but "have decided to follow Jesus and his truth." *Listener E3* listened to AWR online and enjoyed the fundamental teachings program. "Through your radio" says *Listener E3*, "I have decided to join the SDA Church" (Second quarter report, July 23, 2004). Kurt Robert's *First Quarter Report* (August 14, 2007), identified a young man (*Listener E4*) who said his knowledge of

113

Scriptures is limited but he is interested in learning more about God. He therefore requests that the network registers him in their Bible Correspondence Program. While this particular correspondence does not specifically say, I am interested in Adventism; the fact that the individual is asking this religious organization to teach him about God can be seen as openness to learn more about their view of God.

An extensive artifact which is being used in support of "expressed interest in Adventism" is that of a report of a meeting which took place between several SDA Pastors and Administrators in Tanzania, and a Pentecostal Pastor and one of his congregations. The Pentecostal congregation was inspired to observe the seventh-day Sabbath as a result of the broadcasts heard on *Morning Start FM Radio*[2]. According to Nkoko (AWR letters & stories, October 14, 2008), He had the privilege of worshipping with a group of new Sabbath-keepers on September 27, 2008. He and the SDA delegation arrived at the church approximately 10:00a.m. The pastor of the local Pentecostal congregation was standing in the pulpit. He was teaching his congregation about the importance of keeping the fourth commandment, which speaks of the seventh-day Sabbath.

When the SDA delegation was given an opportunity to speak, they shared copies of the denomination's *Sabbath School Daily Lesson Study Guide* which the Pentecostal congregation graciously accepted. The congregation was also introduced to some of the SDA hymns, and was taught how to conduct Sabbath services according to the Adventist tradition. Upon the completion of the worship service which lasted approximately four hours, the SDA delegation met with the Pentecostal pastor and formally interviewed him.

---

[2] Morning Star Radio is owned and operated by Tanzania Union Mission. It started broadcasting in 2003. It currently broadcasts to the Dar es Salaam City, the whole of the Coastal Region and parts of Zanzibar, Morogoro, and Tanga regions.

The pastor talked about his Pentecostal upbringing, his theological studies undertaken in South Korea, and his training in Counseling which was done in the USA. The pastor said he was first introduced to the Ten Commandments and the Sabbath truth while in Germany where he became friends with a successful Jewish businessman. His friend attributed his business and personal success to his strict observance of the Ten Commandments and the observance of the Sabbath in particular. The Pastor said he started observing the Sabbath during his sojourn in the USA and he continued this practice upon his return to Tanzania. This he did privately for over six years, before deciding to share this knowledge and practice with his congregation. When he finally introduced the idea to one of his congregations, the members thought he was confused and a hot debate ensued. This resulted in a rift, and more than 50% of the members withdrew from the fellowship and joined other churches. Of the members remaining, some insisted on continuing the Sunday worship services, while others were open to Sabbath services. He agreed to worship with both factions of his congregation, one group on Sabbath, and the other on Sunday. The pastor credited Morning Star Radio with helping him to convince his church members about the authenticity of the seventh-day Sabbath. The radio broadcasts made it clear to them that Sabbath-keeping was not a strange phenomenon. According to Nkoko (AWR letters & stories, October 14, 2008),

> Morning Star Radio declared to them that there were people around them who were already not only keeping the Sabbath and all the Ten Commandments but also who were economically powerful and successful enough to own and operate a Radio Station. Therefore, they concluded, Sabbath-keeping would not make them a laughing stock. Morning Star Radio became a guiding star in their spiritual journey. (p. 3)

115

The SDA delegation asked the Pentecostal Pastor about some of their practices which were different from that of the Adventists. For example, they wanted to know how he felt about members "falling down and made to experience miraculous healing." The pastor responded in the affirmative, with a response favorable to the Adventists. He quoted various scripture passages which indicated that not everything done in God's name is of God. He emphasized that obeying God's commandments should be foremost, with other manifestations of a relationship with God following as secondary. Following the initial meeting, the Pentecostal pastor was invited to formally record his testimony at the Morning Star Radio station, which he consented to do. The station promised to air his testimony during one of their programs. The group then discussed possible challenges such as that of other SDA members who may not be living up to the truth that they know. The Pentecostal pastor assured the SDA delegation that seeing false witnesses would not deter him because he was well aware that "the devil is at work everywhere." He expressed his belief that there were genuine Sabbath-keepers among Adventists and he wanted to join them. He also wanted to know how he could work for God within the SDA organization.

The SDA delegation encouraged him to continue the work he was engaged in and assured him that they would join him in his efforts to bring all his congregations to a knowledge of the truth, and an observance of the Seventh-day Sabbath. As a follow-up measure, several copies of the *Voice of Prophecy Bible Lesson Guides* were sent to the Pentecostal congregation for them to study as a means of acquainting them with the fundamental teachings of the Seventh-day Adventist Church (R. Nkoko, AWR letters & stories, October 14, 2008).

The AWR headquarters receives quarterly reports from the local studio in Morogoro, as well as from the union office in Tanzania. The studio reports consist of the producers' updates as to the number and nature of correspondences received and activities engaged in since the last report. The reports transmitted from the Union Office focus on the work of the local SDA pastors and lay workers, as well as that of the AWR network. Misiani's report (February 25, 2003), cited a letter received the same day, from the AWR Director in Tanzania. The letter indicated that there was a group of 250 persons in the western part of Tanzania, along Lake Tanganyika, who had been listening to AWR programs and had now expressed their interest in the message and their decision "to accept Christ as their Savior and are keeping the Sabbath." This group of new believers was now in need of more information on what is required to become a Seventh-day Adventist. Misiani indicated that the Secretary/ Treasurer of the West Tanzania Field had been assigned to go and visit them, and that further reports would be given as soon as more feedback was received.

In Kibasisi's report (August 30, 2005) he noted that while attending two camp meetings that summer, he received word that there was a big baptism in the Bagamoyo District, in which 83 Maasai people, including a village chairperson, joined the SDA church. He considered these new converts as "only some apparent fruits of Adventist World Radio." Another account is given of a dialog Kibasisi engaged in with a Maasai warrior who gave a testimony that he was shown in vision that the SDA church was going to do wonderful things in his village and he promised to join the SDA church. The same warrior and his committee also provided the SDA church with a plot of land on which he wanted the SDA Church to build a dispensary, a church building, and a school.

From the artifacts examined, it is evident that multiple channels are used by listeners to convey their interest in learning more about Adventism. Some express their interest via handwritten letters, emails, telephone calls as well as face to face interviews, and messages sent via a third party to the AWR network. Some even express their zeal with tangible gifts. While we cannot judge the motive for the

117

expressed interests, there are several theories and concepts already in place by which these findings can be discussed. The work of Rambo (1993) as expressed in his model of religious conversion, and Rogers' theory of the Diffusion of Innovations (2003) were very instrumental in forming the theoretical framework for this study. In the discussion section which follows, the findings will be discussed according to an amalgamated theoretical framework.

Discussion and Interpretation of Findings

The theoretical framework used to guide the study was that of Rambo's (1993) systematic stage model for understanding the process of religious conversion, and Rogers' (2003) theory on the Diffusion of Innovations. Rambo's model includes seven stages: Context, Crisis, Quest, Encounter, Interaction, Commitment and Consequences. Rogers' theory has four main elements: the innovation, communication channels, the social system, and time. The innovation being examined in this study is that of the religious beliefs of the SDA Church; the channel is that of AWR broadcasts. Time will be discussed in the context of the period of crisis, time spent in questing, and the actual encounters and interactions of the local citizens with missionaries (mechanical or personal). The social system will be comparable to the context in which these encounters, interactions, crises, commitment and ultimately conversion, occur. The following model, Figure 6, was created to illustrate the cyclical nature of the process of conversion and how each element impacts the decision to convert or not to convert.

Each category on the outer circumference of the model has a direct connection to the center. Conversion could occur at anytime, without a potential convert going through all seven stages of the model. The center of the model represents the channel: radio, and the effect: conversion. The encounter stage represents the initial contact of AWR listeners with the radio broadcasts, while the commitment stage represents those who have adopted the new religious ideology as diffused through AWR. The social system represents the context in which the conversion process is played out.

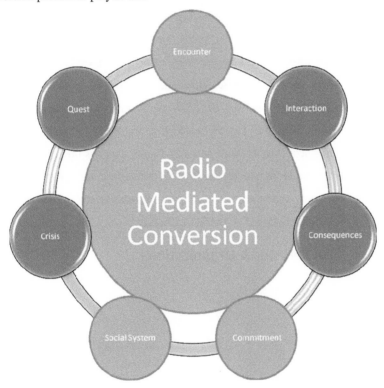

Figure 6: Model depicting conversion as mediated by religious radio broadcasts[3].

---

[3] Note. Model categories derived from Understanding Religious Conversion (p. 18), by L. Rambo, 1993, Yale University, and from Diffusion of Innovations (p. 11), by E. M. Rogers, 2003, NY: Free Press.

The key concepts guiding this study can therefore be seen as cyclical, not sequential with each potential convert having a personal and unique experience, going through the stages at different times, "sometimes going back and forth between the stages" (Rambo, 1993, p. 17). It was clear from the artifacts examined, that the factors contributing to conversion were intertwined. In the case of the SDA Church, AWR was playing a role in the expansion of its membership, but so were the other agencies such as the print media, satellite; educational institutions and medical facilities also operated by the SDA Church. In areas such as the Mara Conference where there were SDA clinics and dispensaries, a secondary school, and access to satellite evangelism, the SDA membership to population ratio was the strongest while the ratio was the weakest in the West Tanzania Field, even though it also had access to the same services. Figure 7 shows the location of SDA services and organizations among the TUM conferences and field. Educational institutions refer only to tertiary and secondary institutions and do not include the primary schools being operated by the SDA Church.

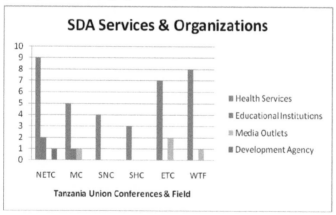

Figure 7: SDA services and organizations located in each SDA Conference

With all conferences within the TUM being exposed to AWR's broadcasts, what accounts for more conversion stories coming from some regions more than others? What are some of the other variables at work? As highlighted in the theoretical framework, other variables include the cultural context, presence or absence of a crisis, the personal innovation tendencies of each individual, the number, duration and type of interactions which occur between missionaries and local citizens, and the consequences of conversion; all these variables impact how willing individuals will be to make a commitment to the new religious ideology presented in the AWR broadcasts. Each of these variables will now be discussed.

Cultural Context

Religious conversion does not occur in a vacuum. There are always multiple channels involved, whether face to face or technology assisted. In this study, the main channel is radio, as used to communicate a religious message. The cultural context of this study is that of the country of Tanzania and how receptive the radio listeners were to the AWR broadcasts. In order to fully understand the setting or cultural context of the conversion process, we need to review briefly Tanzania's history. Germany was the first colonial power to occupy Tanzania and named the country German East Africa. During the 19th century, German missionaries of various faiths sought to convert Tanzanians to their German religions and established various mission posts throughout the country. With the coming of World War II, most of the German missionaries departed. Following the war, British missionaries continued the work started by German missionaries thus establishing denominations such as Catholic, Anglican/Episcopalian, Lutheran, and to a lesser extent, Seventh-day Adventists.

Tanzania was the first east African nation to gain its independence in 1961 and has since been on a path towards self sufficiency adhering somewhat to the principle of Ujamaa or solidarity, as espoused by its first president Mwalimu Nyerere. As is often the case in nation-building, the vision of self-sufficiency was not immediately realized and this resulted in economic challenges for a nation whose economy relied heavily on agriculture. At the formation of the newly independent nation, one of the policies put in place was that of nationalizing the educational and medical facilities that were built and operated by private entities such as religious organizations. But as idealism gave way to economic realities, some of these institutions were returned to the private agencies.

Nyerere's successor, Mwinyi, returned most of the schools and hospitals to their previous owners and created constitutional provisions for the free operation of religion. He viewed religious teachings as important to the moral fiber of the country, and also as a means of correcting erroneous impressions of other faiths (Forster, 1997). With religious organizations now free to teach and evangelize, they had to find ways to "attract" and retain their students. The historic accounts of Vahakangas (2008) highlighted instances in which local groups did not see the value of allowing their children to obtain an education until they noticed that those with an education also had job opportunities, and traveling privileges, which those without an education did not have. The Pew Research Center (2010) noted that Africans were often willing to move from one religious faith to another as deemed essential for educational advancement. Belonging to an international religious organization such as the SDA Church is advantageous as there are educational opportunities worldwide.

Dr. John Kisaka for example, was the first Tanzanian SDA to receive a doctorate in the field of theology, from Andrews University, MI, USA. He became the first principal of the reorganized Tanzania Seminary and College in 1979 (Hoschele, 2007, p. 275). Dr. Kisanga Elineema is another example. He spent the first six months of 1981 in the USA under a Fulbright grant studying the history of the SDA work in his own country of Tanzania. At the time he was employed by the University of Dar es Salaam and was granted leave for his doctoral studies. While in the USA, Elineema was hosted by the staff of the GC Office of Archives and Statistics (Elineema, 1981). Every new SDA believer joins a worldwide network. This access to a global network is a compelling message, especially if there is "perceived popularity" associated with belonging to such a network.

Several scholars have argued that religion is a coping mechanism for those who cannot provide for all their needs. Marx's (1974) theory of religion states that religion allows those who are less fortunate to hope for heaven, as opposed to strive to change their current condition. Hoffer (1963) also argued that those who are poor and frustrated cannot bear reality; therefore possessing faith in God gives them armor with which to fight and to escape the intolerant present. While this is not the case for all new converts in Tanzania, it could be the case for some. The Pew Research Center (2010) found the majority of their Tanzanian respondents being very pessimistic about the economic conditions of the present. Murison (2003) said Tanzania remains one of the poorest nations of the world, with more than one third of its population living below the poverty line. The archival documents analyzed did not portray listeners as being despondent, but their correspondences do suggest that they are open to new ways of viewing the world, and are willing to try new paths on their journey to self improvement. For some listeners the desire for something new could be the outgrowth of a personal or

123

social situation which prompts them to make a change. This leads to yet another variable in the process of religious conversion, that of the inevitability of crises.

Crisis

Rambo (1993) explains that the crisis could be of a personal nature in which the individual feels convicted of wrong doing, acknowledges him or herself as a sinner, needing a Savior; or the crisis could be on a macro level such as a civil war, refugee crises, tribal or ethnic conflict etc. Tanzania shares regional borders with eight countries and has managed to live peacefully with most of its neighbors. The country has been impacted however by a large percentage of its population being refugees from neighboring countries. Relocating can be a challenge, especially if the relocation is forced by the need to survive. While none of the AWR listeners mentioned this experience, their prayer requests covered other types of crises such as sickness, and economic hardships. Rambo (1993) argues that the intensity, duration, scope, nature and source of the crisis will impact the individual's desire for a change and their receptivity for innovative ideas. In the functionalist theory of religion, individuals are open to innovations that help them to make sense of their experiences (Parsons, 1965), therefore a personal crisis may not be obvious to bystanders, but the listener may be able to identify what the driving force was in his or her quest to change their circumstances or to alter their religious beliefs.

Given the number of SDA clinics and dispensaries in operation in Tanzania, it stands to reason that there may be several cases of medical crises which could be revealed if an ethnographic approach was included as a part of the methodology for this study. The medical work of the SDA Church is a strong arm in its evangelism efforts. As was cited in the findings to research question # 1e, a Maasai warrior who expressed an interest in becoming an Adventist presented the SDA Church

124

with a gift in the form of acres of land. He expressed his desire for the SDA Church to build a dispensary, a church, and a school on the same site. Embedded in his gift is the stipulation for his people to be educated, be able to receive medical treatment, as well as have a place for worship and fellowship.

In the Pew Research Center's study (2010) it was noted that across the East Africa region, many people struggle to afford the basic necessities of life. It was therefore up to religious organizations to provide relief and development for the needy, especially if the government is unable to do so. While the literature reviewed showed several cases of the Tanzanian government partnering with other entities to provide family planning education and resources etc. the literature also showed that the government recognized the value of religious organizations in helping to meet the needs of its citizens. Not only does the SDA Church provide medical assistance, educational opportunities and religious programming, but it also provides development and relief in times of crises such as that experienced by orphans in the *Cradle of Love Baby Home*. The Adventist Development and Relief Agency (ADRA) operate in a somewhat similar way to the Red Cross in that it is a first responder wherever there is a disaster or developmental need. With an ADRA regional office located in Arusha, Tanzania, it is fair to conclude that the SDA Church has a visible presence in Tanzania and would be ready and willing to assist in the event of a national crisis. The AWR network would also become a channel through which emergency assistance information would be provided.

The next element of the theoretical framework to be discussed is three fold: We will examine the nature of the encounters between missionaries and local citizens, the type of interactions they engage in and the quest that fuels these activities.

125

Quest, Encounters, and Interactions

AWR listeners who request more information about SDA beliefs, or request enrollment in the Bible Correspondence Programs are involved in "active questing," meaning they are deliberately in search of new innovative religious ideas, based on new found dissonance with their previous views. Those listeners who enjoy programming related to marriage principles, and secrets of success, as well as programs that teach fundamental SDA doctrines are exhibiting a "receptive" response. Other forms of response noted by Rambo include "rejecting": those consciously rejecting the new option; "apathetic": those who have no interest in a new religious option; or a "passive response" as demonstrated by those who are so weak and in need that they could be manipulated by external circumstances (Rambo, 1993, p. 59).

Curiosity is a built-in trait for all humans. Some will be more adventurous than others, hence Rogers (2003) was able to create a continuum for those who are innovators, early adopters, those who would adopt a new idea when the majority did (majority adopters), late adopters and laggards, those who would simply be the last to embrace anything other than the traditional norm. Whatever the rate of adoption, it begins with a quest, a desire for something new or different. Rambo (1993) identified at least five different modes of response once the new innovations (SDA ideology in AWR broadcasts) are encountered. Tanzanian radio listeners encountering the AWR broadcasts can therefore choose an "active, receptive, rejecting, apathetic or passive response" (Rambo, 1993, p. 59).

None of the listener correspondences reviewed reflected any apathetic, passive or rejecting responses; though that does not mean they did not exist. Other literature reviewed indicated that there were instances of "rejecting responses." *News Notes* (March 2, 1978) reported a story of a radio broadcast which reversed a rejecting response. The author noted that a witnessing class in one of the villages had difficulty in its house to house visits until they heard an SDA preacher on Radio Tanzania. At first the residents thought that Adventism was prohibited, but when they heard the SDA pastor on the radio they concluded that the new religion must be safe as the government allowed them to use the airwaves.

According to Hoschele (2007a), even the missionaries disagreed at times as to how cultural differences should be addressed:

The Adventist missionaries advocated that a polygamous man should leave all his wives except one. This decision brought several problems. Thus a polygamist who embraced Christianity often chose to postpone baptism until all his wives save one had passed away, or else he disowned them on his deathbed in order to be baptized. Still others disowned their wives only to join them again after becoming church members. (p. 300)

According to Elineema (1995), the SDA Church also frowned upon "initiation rites." When it was discovered that an SDA girl had been initiated, she was censored, and sent to worship with another congregation for a predetermined probationary period. Such practices could have resulted in some "apathetic" responses. While the AWR listener correspondences sampled cannot be a predictor of gender percentages within the SDA Church of Tanzania, it was interesting to note that 44% of correspondents identified themselves as males, while only 6% identified as females. The specific gender of the other 50% could not be determined.

Rambo (1993) argued that we often hear of the thousands who respond favorably, but very little mention is ever made of the larger percentage of the population who do not respond favorably. Gabbert (2001) noted in his research that the requirement of having one spouse was a major deterrent to conversion as polygamy was wide-spread in Tanzania. In order for Tanzanians to receive baptism

127

into the Moravian faith, they had to be separated from their husbands. More women accepted this injunction more than men, resulting in the majority of converts being female. In the 1930s, women outnumbered men. The church had more leadership and advancement opportunities for women, therefore the women felt that they had much to gain in joining the church. The men on the other hand felt like they had much to lose therefore many did not convert until they were on their death beds.

Education has been a first point of encounter for many new religious converts. According to Elineema (1995), the SDA Church operated 192 temporary and permanent primary schools between 1905 and 1963 when the primary schools were nationalized. By 1995, the SDA Church operated only 10 secondary schools and a college. During the early years of Adventism in Tanzania (1931), the SDA Church was credited with graduating the first certified female teacher in the country, prompting the Director of Education to congratulate the SDA Church for "having established an important landmark in the progress of female education" (Elineema, 1995, p. 56).

The encounters and interactions that have occurred through the years are all instrumental in the SDA Church's achievement of its mission; every positive encounter, leads to more encounters. Eventually, potential converts become willing to move into a secluded compound for educational and or vocational pursuits. While the interactions of AWR listeners with AWR personnel are usually brief, their interactions with local SDA personnel will be more expansive as they are usually responsible to carry out the face to face follow-up visits. Positive interactions developed via correspondences can also serve as a fore-runner to the face to face interactions. The listeners often wait extended periods of time before they are able to put a face with the name or voice they had become attached to during their period of listening and corresponding with the AWR network.

Once listeners have participated in the quest stage, and have encountered and interacted with SDA personnel for some time, there comes a point in the relationship when certain decisions have to be made; consequences are assessed, commitments are made, and an evaluation of the conversion process occurs.

Commitments, Consequences and Conversion

All religious movements go through seasons of growth, stagnation and decline. Individuals like to be a part of organizations that are moving in a favorable direction. Duke and Johnson (1989) formulated a macro-sociological theory of religion. They argued that higher rates of conversion usually occur during growth and peak seasons of dominance, as opposed to periods of apostasy and decline. It is not always possible to discern the motive of those who decide to join the movement, but time is usually a good indicator of the strength of the commitment. The SDA Church has experienced years of sustained growth in the Tanzania Union Mission of SDA. Table 2 shows the increasing trend in membership within the six conferences and field, since the inception of Maasai language programs in 2001. The table was created with information gathered from the 138th Annual Statistical Report (2001) to the 146th Annual Statistical Report (2008). The Annual Statistical Reports are compiled by the SDA Office of Archives and Statistics located in Silver Spring, MD.

129

Table 2: Statistical Report Showing SDA Membership per Year within Tanzania Union Mission Conferences: 2000-2008.

Conferences	2000	2001	2002	2003	2004	2005	2006	2007	2008
North East	46,778	56,977	62,025	66,343	69,859	71,595	74,347	77,122	76,925
Mara	63,864	68,891	69,908	75,284	80,771	84,898	87,647	93,810	100,650
South Nyanza	66,312	71,890	75,327	82,078	86,411	92,560	96,346	101,921	106,523
South West	19,553	20,884	21,656	22,641	22,628	23,637	25,446	26,417	28,291
East	25,409	31,373	34,537	39,008	36,172	42,774	49,263	52,746	58,367
West	18,685	20,200	21,645	22,251	24,802	26,545	30,220	32,668	36,094
Total Membership	240,601	270,215	285,098	307,604	320,643	342,009	363,269	384,684	406,850

The three incidents of decline (as underlined in table), represent temporary dips in the overall membership numbers which continue to have an upward trajectory according to the 2009 statistical reports (Jones & Proctor, 2009). The Maasai language programs were described as the "air assault" needed to pave the way for the "foot soldiers" to come after. Other imagery used by the Maasai language program producer included "a harvest of souls," and Maasai mass baptisms were described as the "first fruits" of many more to follow if AWR is able to increase the number of hours the programs are on the air, as well as increase the number of workers assigned to do follow-up visits. The program producer lamented being the only person preparing the programs and also going out to do follow-up visits. He described the situation in Biblical terms saying that the harvest was ripe but the laborers were few.

Admission into SDA Church membership is usually granted after three prerequisites are met. The first is conversion, followed by an acceptance of the principles and doctrines of the SDA Church, and thirdly, baptism by immersion. Those complying with these prerequisites are granted membership by vote of the members. For those requesting admission by baptism, the vote may be taken prior to baptism (that is "subject to baptism") or after baptism. Those requesting membership who were previously baptized by immersion may be received on "profession of their faith." In this category are those who were members of other denominations that practice baptism by immersion, and who wish to be received on their former baptisms.

The SDA Church also has policies related to transferring of memberships or withdrawal of the "right hand of fellowship." While accessions are not desirable, they are a natural part of the process. From a global perspective, the SDA Church baptized more than five million people in a five year period, but lost nearly 1.4 million during that same period of time (GC SDA Church: Conserving Gains-An Appeal, 2010). Some of the losses were attributed to deaths, while others included apostasy, or withdrawal and non-reporting. The SDA Church is so concerned about the number of converts who withdraw from its fellowship that it has issued the following statement:

> Research on why members leave the SDA Church fellowship suggests that social and relational factors are much more significant than disagreement with denominational teachings. In fact, many who leave denominational fellowship remain supportive of SDA beliefs and even maintain church practices for some time following their departure...The reasons most frequently cited by persons who leave are found in the realm of relationships, the absence of a sense of belonging, and the lack of meaningful engagement in the local congregation and its mission. Therefore, the loss of membership for these reasons should be preventable. (GC SDA Church: Conserving membership gains-An appeal, 2010).

Rambo (1993) created several hypotheses about the dynamics of conversion. Three of them were presented in the review of literature and restated as follows: Cultures that are stable, resilient and effective will have very few members willing

131

to abandon their place in that culture to join another. Secondly, a strong culture will reward those who stay in place and punish those who leave, and thirdly, if the culture is experiencing a crisis, it will be more tempting for members to leave. The same could be said of religious movements. If new converts become enmeshed into the new way of life, establish close knit relationships and feel like they belong, accession would be less likely.

On the other hand, it is necessary to leave room for reversions and growth. Post-dissonance will exist whenever individuals have made a life changing decision. At times the decision to convert may include estrangement from family and friends who are not in agreement with the decision. Rambo (1993) contends that this "inner resolve to shift loyalties is never complete; old urges return, sometimes with greater power than before" (p. 136). Religious groups that make allowances for these post decision conflicts tend to retain more of their members as opposed to more conservative groups that expect the old ways to die and remain buried.

Many scholars question the authenticity of the conversion process. Some question the motive and rationale for converting; others question what types of incentives are given as enticements. It is a phenomenon that requires continued study. This researcher concurs with Rambo (1993) that the process is complicated; it is both elusive and inclusive; it can be sudden and or gradual; it is personal and communal, private and public (p. 176). What this study reinforced is that conversion is a process impacted by many variables. While the contributions of AWR are duly noted, especially where it is credited with influencing mass baptisms among the Maasai people, it is also evident that AWR's broadcasts are but one of many factors contributing to the spread of SDA ideology in the Tanzania Union Mission of the Seventh-day Adventist Church.

132

CHAPTER 6: CONCLUSION

The goal of this study was to determine the extent of a cause and effect relationship between the Seventh-day Adventist (SDA) church's media usage in east-central Africa, and the growth of the SDA church in Tanzania. The historical systematic methodology was used to analyze various artifacts such as listener correspondences, studio reports, minutes, memos, letters, publications etc, related to the work of the SDA Church in Tanzania, East Central Africa. The East Central Africa Division (ECD) is the second largest of the 13 SDA world divisions and covers the countries of Burundi, Democratic Republic of Congo (DRC), Djibouti, Eritrea, Ethiopia, Kenya, Rwanda, Somalia, Tanzania, and Uganda. Tanzania was the first east African country to receive SDA missionaries in 1903, but the SDA membership within Tanzania today, falls behind that of Kenya, and DRC. The Tanzania Union Mission (TUM) was organized in 1903 and reorganized in 1960. Its current SDA membership to population ratio is 1:97.

This study asked one overarching question: *To what extent has Adventist World Radio succeeded in fulfilling the Seventh-day Adventist Church's mission within the Tanzania Union Mission of Seventh-day Adventists?* As the study findings and discussion have shown, to declare the mission a success would be to declare all "un-entered territories" as "entered" and this is not yet the case. The gospel is being preached into the entire world. The SDA Yearbook (2010) records 232 countries as recognized by the United Nations, with an established SDA work in 203 of those countries. This represents 87.5% of the world that is currently exposed to Adventism. The SDA Church is methodical and systematic in its strategic planning and mission to present the gospel to the whole world. The data

133

show that all the church's media organizations, ministries, and services are operated with that mission in mind.

Broadcast languages are constantly being added to the AWR schedule to ensure that many nations, kindred, tongue and people are able to hear the message in a native language. There are currently 80 languages being used in AWR broadcasts (AWR 2011), while the SDA printing presses currently utilize 369 different languages in their publications (SDA Yearbook, 2010), including Kiswahili and Maasai, as spoken in Tanzania. The SDA Church has engaged in the publication of Bible translations and hymnal creations to nurture faith and nourish hope in the Second Advent, as preached by the denomination. As early as 1911, a song book and the gospel of Matthew were translated into Chasu, the language of the Pare people in north east Tanzania (Hoschele, 2003).

Listeners have expressed their appreciation for the programs being aired on AWR and are doing their part in extending the reach of the AWR network by creating listening circles in their neighborhoods with loud speakers attached to their radios. Findings were presented of a Pentecostal Pastor who was seeking to convert his congregations to Adventism, and the SDA Church delegation was very receptive to the idea. Listeners have demonstrated their commitment to the new ideology diffused via the radio channel, and over time they have made financial contributions (based on the amount of money given for tithes and offerings), as well as donations in kind, such as the gift of land. While all the names were not known and all the stories could not be told, there is sufficient evidence to provide a richer explanation than would have been possible had this study not been undertaken.

Limitations

This study was limited methodologically, geographically, and historically. Methodologically, this study focused on the historical systematic method which allowed for an examination of artifacts left by the past. Other methods of analysis which could be explored include a rhetorical criticism of the actual radio programs. Distance, time and funding were also inhibiting factors. More time would have allowed for the expansion of the research protocol, complete with confidentiality statements from human subjects. With additional time and funding for international travel, the researcher would be able to visit the geographic region and conduct interviews with some of the actual listeners and program producers. In-depth interviews would then be used to supplement what the historical records were able to reveal.

Geographically, the study focused on only one east African country, that of the Republic of Tanzania. A more comparative assessment could be done if other east African countries with a similar level of exposure to AWR broadcasts were examined as well. Kenya for example, shares borders with Tanzania, with the Maasai residing on both sides of the border. This artificial demarcation excluded from this analysis, artifacts related to the Maasai in Kenya. The researcher also gathered extensive material for all 10 east African countries belonging to the East Central Africa Division of SDA. A recommendation therefore is that of extending this study beyond the current limitations to include discussion and analysis of the findings for the other countries as well.

Examining the religious affiliations of AWR listeners is another research project that could be developed. Are there other evangelical or Protestant groups

135

that share similar religious beliefs that may also be actively listening to the AWR broadcasts, or conducting their own broadcasts? Several of the studio reports from Morogoro, Tanzania mentioned other religious groups who were listening to the programs and engaging in follow-up visits, discussing the Bible topics covered, and leading listeners to become members of other denominations. Rather than perceiving this as a competition for souls, this could become a great opportunity for collaborative efforts leading to a clearer understanding of the Biblical principles being studied. A more specific research question related to this potential study would be that of examining AWR's influence among non-SDA ministers. Some of the documents reviewed in the course of this study identified Pentecostal as well as Baptist ministers who were interested in learning more about Adventism, and possibly bringing entire congregations with them. Listener conferences could also be conducted in various regions to allow for face to face dialog with those who have been involved in this type of media related conversion. More studies need to be done to access the contributions AWR is making to the growth of the SDA Church in other countries as well.

From a historical perspective, the scope of this study covered only the first 25 years of AWR-Africa. A longitudinal study, per AWR network, or by broadcast languages, would create a fuller picture of the periods of membership growth, stagnation and decline since the inception of the radio network. More triangulation would also make greater allowances for a deeper analysis of the roles played by other variables through the years. Despite these limitations however, there are some significant contributions that this study can make.

Implications

This study has the capacity to make contributions in the expansion of theories related to religious communication. It also serves to expand the body of knowledge currently available in academe. The theoretical contribution of this study rests on the fact that the researcher was able to utilize an old systematic stage model on the process of religious conversion (Rambo, 1993), combined with that of the more widely known Diffusion of Innovation (DOI) theory to study the dissemination of SDA religious ideas across the Tanzanian culture, through the medium of radio. This usage is in addition to the many ways in which the theory of the Diffusion of Innovations has been used in the past. In 1962 when the DOI theory was originally created, the purpose was to study the diffusion of agricultural innovations. Since then several studies have been conducted utilizing this theory in various ways but to date, no study has been identified in which the DOI theory was used to study the spread of religious ideology across cultures.

The innovation addressed in this study is that of Adventism as presented via AWR-Africa broadcasts in the country of Tanzania. Adventism began in North America during the 1860s and has since expanded to over 200 countries of the world (Jones & Proctor, 2010). Today the largest proportions of the 16 million Adventists live outside of North America with East-Central Africa being ranked second in percentage of church members. In response to Rogers' (2003) argument that we do not need more-of-the-same diffusion research, this research accepted the challenge to "move beyond the proven methods of the past" (Rogers, 2003, p. xxi) to achieve theoretical significance in its application of the diffusion of innovations theory, thereby broadening its conceptions.

Another area in which this study makes a contribution is its potential for practical application. There are hundreds of religious broadcasting networks around the world but despite the growing trend of missionaries utilizing radio to spread a religious message, very few studies have been conducted in the area of international religious radio broadcasting. The findings of this case study therefore will be practical for the SDA Church as it will provide an analysis of the work of one of its institutions within one division of the world church. This could then serve as a baseline for the analysis of the work of AWR worldwide, as well as provide a comparative assessment for many other international religious broadcasting entities. By utilizing a single instrumental case study (Stake, 1995), the researcher was able to focus on an issue or concern, and then select one bounded case to illustrate this issue.

Thirdly, this study adds to the body of knowledge currently available in academia about religion and mass communication. More specifically, media usage and their effect, the work of international religious broadcasting in east Africa, and the process of conversion as mediated through radio. With no study identified focusing on the role of international religious broadcasting in international church growth and expansion, this study was not a replication of any other study. Instead the study took an original approach in order to expand the body of knowledge available in the sphere where media and religion unite within the geographic region of East-Central Africa. The study also has heuristic potential in that its case study approach can be replicated for other religious networks, thereby stimulating more research in this area. This study was also an example of serendipity at work, in that there were a few instances in which the researcher gained insights more valuable than what was actually being sought.

138

Conclusion

The SDA Church's mission involves the proclamation of the Christian message for the building of a community of believers who keep the commandments of God and have the faith of Jesus (Rev. 14:12). The driving mission of the SDA Church is that of the Christian message being preached to every nation, kindred, tongue and people, as outlined in Revelation 14. The SDA Church is constantly expanding its outreach initiatives to include broadcasts and publications in multiple languages, as well as sending missionaries into regions that do allow for them to work within their chosen career fields. The SDA Church's organizational structure allows for international assistance to be provided in regions that are unable to carry out the Church's mission on their own.

The studio reports from Tanzania include several requests for more workers doing face to face visitations in response to the AWR broadcasts. The AWR staff was unable to fulfill in a timely manner, all the requests brought to their attention. Requests for literacy classes to be conducted in Maasai communities were also presented. In the words of Kibasisi (AWR letters & stories, December 13, 2004), literacy classes for both children and adults would aid the Maasai people in reading the Bible for themselves.

The AWR network also provides technical assistance to the studio operations in Morogoro, Tanzania. In AWR letters and stories (December 13, 2004), it was noted that a "digital editing and producer training course" was provided to facilitate digital and professional production in the AWR studio in Morogoro. A local FM station "Morning Star Radio" has been in operation in Tanzania since 2003. As more local stations come into operation, the demand or dependence on the international network will decrease. At the launch of the Morning Star FM Radio station, the President of the SDA world church was in attendance where a

139

crowd of more than 30,000 packed the venue. Dr. Jan Paulsen was able to dedicate the facility, along with a new multipurpose building which was constructed to house a church, and a conference hall complete with guest rooms and a kitchen (ANN report, December 2, 2003). This is another example of the multidimensional approach of the SDA Church.

Nurturing believers in preparation for Jesus' return is also a part of the SDA Church's mission. Ideas of how the nurturing should be done are as varied as the many cultures represented within the SDA Church. The Maasai language program producer showcased some of the activities that non-SDA Church's have engaged in as a means of suggesting that the SDA Church expands its efforts in Tanzania. Kibasisi (AWR letters & stories, December 13, 2004) cited the Lutheran Church which built a high school for Maasai girls in a traditional Maasai Manyata design. The Manyata design is circular, with huts built around a cattle enclosure. The Lutheran Church used that concept to build their church in the center and the school classrooms surrounding the church.

Another suggestion made by Kibasisi for nurturing believers, was that of building a Maasai fashioned TV, Radio and Education Center. He foresaw this as a means of reaching the world. He described it as:

> ...an open door for millions all over the world to hear and watch, that which is a tourist attraction in East Africa. Since the world appreciates Maasai culture, the church could make it available. A few SDA Maasai who are multilingual could serve as speakers presenting God's word with original culture. (AWR letters & stories, December 13, 2004)

All the SDA Church Yearbooks reviewed, prominently feature the church's mission: proclaiming the message to the world; the method: through preaching, teaching and healing; and the vision: to see the complete restoration of God's perfect creation. This study revealed that AWR is an integral part of the SDA

Church's global ministry and the network is doing its part to fulfill the Church's objective in spreading the Adventist message around the world.

REFERENCES

Primary/ Archival Sources

Adventist World Radio (1981). Minutes of various elements of AWR 1981-1993. (Record Identification No.13351: 102). Silver Spring, MD: Office of Archives and Statistics.

Adventist World Radio (1985). Correspondence of AWR, 1985-1988. (Record Identification No.13352: 102). Silver Spring, MD: Office of Archives and Statistics.

Adventist World Radio (1988). News clippings, 1988-1990. (Record Identification No.13344: 102). Silver Spring, MD: Office of Archives and Statistics.

Adventist World Radio (1990). Comments from listeners' letters, compiled April 5, 1990.(Record Identification No.10302: 102). Silver Spring, MD: Office of Archives and Statistics.

Adventist World Radio (1991). Adventist World Radio worker monitor reports. (Record Identification No.13361: 102). Silver Spring, MD: Office of Archives and Statistics.

Adventist World Radio (1993). Information requests 1993 to 1999. (Record

Identification No.13359: 102). Silver Spring, MD: Office of Archives and Statistics.

Adventist World Radio (1994a). Listener mail, 1994 to March 1995. (Record Identification No.13343: 102). Silver Spring, MD: Office of Archives and Statistics.

Adventist World Radio (1994b). A brief history, the Voice of Hope for all peoples. (Record Identification No.10304: 102). Silver Spring, MD: Office of Archives and Statistics.

Adventist World Radio (1995a). Listener mail, April 1995 to 1997. (Record Identification No.13344: 102). Silver Spring, MD: Office of Archives and Statistics.

Adventist World Radio (1995b). Just the facts: broadcasting the three angels messages since 1971. (Record Identification No.10301: 102). Silver Spring, MD: Office of Archives and Statistics.

Adventist World Radio (1999a). A brief history: Voice of Prophecy. (Record Identification No.10305: 102). Silver Spring, MD: Office of Archives and Statistics.

Adventist World Radio (1999b). General facts and information. (Record Identification No.10303: 102). Silver Spring, MD: Office of Archives and Statistics.

Adventist World Radio (2001). 30 years of Adventist World Radio (calendar). (Record Identification No.14172: 102). Silver Spring, MD: Office of Archives and Statistics.

Adventist World Radio (2007, March 26). Broadcast coverage. Retrieved February 11, 2008, from http://www.awr2.org/index.php?option=com_content&task=view&id=12&Itemid=12.

Adventist World Radio (2007, March 26). Mission and Organization. Retrieved February 11, 2008, from http://www.awr2.org/index.php?option=com_content&task=view&id=12&Itemid=12.

Adventist World Radio (2010, February). Official broadcast languages. Silver Spring, MD:AWR main office, General Conference of Seventh-day Adventists.

Adventist Word Radio (2011). Broadcasts. Retrieved March 22, 2011 from http://www.awr.org/en/about_awr/broadcasts.

Adventist World Radio (n.d.).: Collection of documents showing its history and development [1971- 1996]. (File Folder # 008104). Berrien Springs, MI: Center for Adventist Research, Andrews University.

Adventist World Radio (n.d.). Inventory listing of 24-box collection. (Record

Identification No.13343: 102). Silver Spring, MD: Office of Archives and Statistics.

Adventist World Radio (n.d.). Coverage map and mission Statement (Record Identification No.7969: 102). Silver Spring, MD: Office of Archives and Statistics.

Cook, A. E. (1967, March). Tanzania Union: "Bring wood-build the house." *Trans-Africa Division Outlook, 65* (3), p. 4. Retrieved from http://www.adventistarchives.org.

Davy, A L. (1963, January). Tanganyika Union. *Southern African Division Outlook, 61*(1), p. 24. Retrieved from http://www.adventistarchives.org.

Freesland, S. N. (2005, Autumn). Taking the gospel to the Maasai. *Transmissions, 4.*

GC: Adventist World Radio (2001a, December). Adventist World Radio Africa report for The Africa-Indian-Ocean Division. Historical material (Record Identification No.0000054: 104157: 04250: Box number 6052: S744). Silver Spring, MD: Office of Archives and Statistics.

GC: Adventist World Radio (2001b, December). Listener mail: Listener letters – Africa. (Record Identification No.0000022: 104137: 04250: Box number 6050: S743). Silver Spring, MD: Office of Archives and Statistics.

GC: Adventist World Radio (2001c, December). Files listed by country, 1985 to

2001 (J to Z). (Record Identification No.0000040: 104132: 04250: Box number 6049: S742). Silver Spring, MD: Office of Archives and Statistics.

General Conference of Seventh-day Adventists (2010). *Roadmap for Mission—A new policy A 20.* Retrieved April 28, 2010 from http://www.adventist.org/beliefs/other_documents/roadmap.html.

General Conference of Seventh-day Adventists (2010). *Conserving membership gains— An appeal.* Retrieved April 28, 2010 from http://www.adventist.org/beliefs/other_documents/conserving-gains.html.

Henning, R. H. (1970, June). New office building for Tanzania General Field. *Trans-Africa Division Outlook, 68* (6), p. 8. Retrieved from http://www.adventistarchives.org.

Henning, R. H. (1969, June). "Ye are my witnesses". *Trans-Africa Division Outlook, 67*(6), p. 9. Retrieved from http://www.adventistarchives.org.

Kisaka, J. A. (1970a, June). The historic Masai [sic] baptism. *Trans-Africa Division Outlook, 68* (6), p. 5. Retrieved from http://www.adventistarchivs.org on August 12, 2010.

Kisaka, J. A. (1970b, August). Tanzania: First three baptized from Masai [sic] tribe. *Review and Herald, 147* (39), p. 16. Retrieved from http://www.adventistarchives.org on August 12, 2010.

Marx, R. D. (1968). The gospel penetrates the cities of Tanzania. *Missions*

Quarterly, 57 (4), 14-16.

Masokomya, F. (1957, January 15). The wings of the three angels' messages. *Southern African Division Outlook, 55* (1), pp. 10, 11. Retrieved from http://www.adventistarchives.org.

News notes from the world divisions (1978). Afro-Mideast. *Adventist Review, 155* (09), p. 28.

Schoun, B. (2005, Autumn). Message from the president: Dear sharers in AWR's mission. *Transmissions*, 3.

Werner, P. G. (1966, September). A time for advance in Tanzania. Review and Herald,143 (4), p. 16-19. Retrieved from http://www.adventistarchives.org. August 12, 2010.

Secondary Sources

Babbie, E. (2007). *The practice of social research (11ᵗʰ ed.).* CA: Thomson Wadsworth.

Bertoncini, E. Z. (1989). *Outline of Swahili literature.* London: E. J. Brill.

Bullet, R. (1979). *Conversion to Islam in the medieval period: An essay in quantitative history.* Cambridge, MA: Harvard University Press.

Burger, P. L. & Luckmann, T. (1969). Sociology of religion and sociology of knowledge in Robertson, R. (1969). (Ed.). *Sociology of religion.* Harmondsworth: Penguin.

Carpenter, J. A. & Shenk, W. R. (1990). (Eds.), *Earthen vessels: American evangelicals and foreign missions, 1880-1980.* Grand Rapids, MI: William B. Eerdmans publishing company.

Chaffee, S. H. (1992). Search for change: Survey studies of international media effects. In F. Korzenny & S. Ting-Toomey (Eds.), *Mass media effects across cultures* (pp. 35-54). CA: Sage.

Chang, B., Lee, S. & Kim, B. (2006). Exploring factors affecting the adoption and continuance of online games among college students in South Korea: Integrating uses and gratification and diffusion of innovation approaches. *New Media & Society, 8* (2), 295-319.

Creswell, J. W. (2007). *Qualitative Inquiry & Research Design: Choosing Among Five Approaches. (2nd ed.).* Thousand Oaks, CA: Sage Publications, Inc.

Creswell, J. W. (1994). *Research design: Qualitative & quantitative approaches.* CA: Sage Publications.

De Witte, M. (2003). Altar media's living word: Televised charismatic Christianity in Ghana. *Journal of Religion in Africa, 33* (2), 172-202.

Duke, J. T. & Johnson, B. L. (1989). The stages of religious transformation: A study of 200 nations. *Review of Religious Research 30,* 209-224.
148

Durkheim, E. (1961). *The elementary forms of the religious life*. NY: Collier Books.

Elineema, K. B. (Ed.). (1995). The development of the Seventh-day Adventist Church in Tanzania, (pp. 44-63). *In Proceedings of the international scientific symposium on the development of the SDA Church in Eastern Africa: Past, present and future*. Dar es Salaam, Tanzania: Dar es Salaam University Press.

Elineema, K. B. (1981). Tanzania: A triumph of faith. *Adventist Review, 158* (33), p. 16, 17.

Forster, P. G. (1997). Religion and the state of Tanzania and Malawi. *Journal of Asian & African Studies (Brill), 32,* (3/4), 163-185.

Freedom House (2010). Freedom in the world 2010: Erosion of freedom intensifies. Retrieved April 15, 2010 from http://www.freedomhouse.org.

Fulk, J. (1993). Social construction of communication technologies. *Academy of Management Journal 36* (5), 921-50.

Gabbert, W. (2001). Social and cultural conditions of religious conversion in colonial southwest Tanzania, 1891-1939. *Ethnology 40* (4), 291-308.

Hale, J. (1975). *Radio power: Propaganda and international broadcasting*. Philadelphia: Temple University Press.
149

Haralambos, M. and Holborn, M. (1990). *Sociology themes and perspectives. (3rd ed.).* London: Unwin Hyman Ltd.

Head, S.W., Sterling, C. H., & Schofield, L. B. (1994). *Broadcasting in America: A survey of Electronic media.* Boston: Houghton Mifflin Company.

Hoffer, E. (1963). *The true believer.* NY: Time Incorporated.

Hoschele, S. (2007a). Religious critique discourses as community quarrels: Friction of values as expressed by Tanzanian Adventists. *Religion & Theology 14*, 244-264.

Hoschele, S. (2007b). *Christian remnant- African folk church: Seventh-Day Adventism in Tanzania, 1903-1980.* The Netherlands: Brill.

Hoschele, S. (2003). *Centennial album of the Seventh-day Adventist Church in Tanzania: Pictures from our history 1903-2003.* Arusha, Tanzania: Tanzania Union of Seventh-day Adventists.

Howell, M. & Prevenier, W. (2001). *From reliable sources: Introduction to historical methods.* Ithaca: Cornell University Press.

Hughes, R. D. (1980). *The role of broadcasting in the contextualization of the gospel in sub- Saharan Africa.* Available from ProQuest Works and Theses database. (UMI No. 8018646)

Infante, D. A., Rancer, A. S., & Womack, D. F. (1997). *Building communication theory (3rd ed.)*. Illinois: Waveland Press, Inc.

Iverson, H. R. (1984). *Case studies in the Christian ministry in Ujamaa: Sonjo-the shortcoming of approaches to mission and Boay-the emergent African Church*. Paper presented at the Conference Religion, Development and African Identity, Uppsala, 16-21 August 1984, Scandinavian Institute of African Studies, Nordic Institute for missiology and ecumenical research.

Kane, J. H. (1981). *The Christian world mission: Today and tomorrow*. Grand Rapids, MI: Baker Book House.

Kisaka, J. A. (1995). The global strategies: The case of Tanzania, (pp.189-199). In *Proceedings of the international scientific symposium on the development of the SDA Church in Eastern Africa: Past, present and future*. (Elineema, K. B. (Ed.). Dar es Salaam, Tanzania: Dar es Salaam University Press.

Korzenny, F., & Schiff, E. (1992). Media effects across cultures: Challenges and opportunities. In F. Korzenny & S. Ting-Toomey (Eds.). *Mass media effects across cultures* (pp. 1-8). CA: Sage.

Kruisheer, K. (1999). Nani alionja nini? Who had a taste of what? A sociopolitical interpretation of Farouk Topan's play Aliyeonja pepo ("A Taste of Heaven"), Dar es Salaam, 1973. *Research in African Literatures, 30*, (1), 44-57.

Kushner, J. M. (1976). *International religious radio broadcasting in Africa:*

Program policies and problem areas. Available from ProQuest Works and Theses database. (UMI No. 7709964).

Laswell, H. D. (1948). The structure and function of communication in society. In L. Bryson (Ed.), *The communication of ideas* (pp. 37-51). New York: Harper.

Lazarsfeld, P. F. & Stanton, F. N. (1944). *Radio research 1942-1943.* New York: Duel, Sloan, and Pearce.

Leonard, R. (2003, September 19). From Gutenberg to the Web, church's media savvy waxes and wanes. *National Catholic Reporter, 33.*

Ligaga, D. (2005). Narrativising development in radio drama: Tradition and realism in the Kenyan radio play Ushikwapo Shikamana. *Social Identities, 11* (2), 131-145.

Malinowski, B. (1954). *Magic, science and religion and other essays.* New York: Anchor Books.

Mano, W. (2004). Renegotiating tradition on radio Zimbabwe. *Media, Culture & Society, 26,* (3), 315-336.

Martin, J. P. (1998). Christianity and Islam: Lessons from Africa. *Brigham Young University Law Review, 1998 (2)*, 401-421.

Marx, K. (1974). *Capitol,* vol. III. London: Lawrence & Wishart.

McQuail, D. (1984). With the benefit of hindsight: Reflections on uses and gratifications research. *Critical Studies in Mass Communication, 1*, 177-93.

Midgley, D. F. & Dowling, R. G. (1978). Innovativeness-concept and its measurement, *Journal of Consumer Research 4* (4), 229-42.

Morris, M.W., Leung, K., Ames, D., & Lickel, B. (1999). Views from inside and outside: Integrating emic and etic insights about culture and justice judgment. *Academy of Management Review, 24* (4), 781-796.

Niblo, D. M. & Jackson, M.S. (2004). Model for combining the qualitative emic approach with the quantitative derived etic approach. *Australian Psychologist, 39* (2), 127-133.

Nutini, H. (1988). *Todos Santos in rural Tlaxcala*. Princeton.

Parsons, T. (1965). Religious perspectives in sociology and social psychology in Lessa, W. A. and Vogt, E. Z. (1965). *Reader in comparative religion: an anthropological approach. (2nd ed.)*. New York: Harper & Row.

Perry, S. H. (2003). Resolving conflict through solar-powered radio in Chad. *Journal of Women in Culture and Society, 29, (2) 561-564.*

Potkanski, T. & Adams, W. M. (1998). Water scarcity, property, regimes and irrigation management in Sonjo, Tanzania. *The Journal of Development Studies, 34*, (4), 86-116.

Rambo, L. R. (1993). *Understanding religious conversion*. New Haven and London: Yale University Press.

Razafimbelo-Harisoa, M. S. (2005). Radio in Madagascar: roles and missions. *The Radio Journal-International Studies in Broadcast and Audio Media, 3* (1), 35-44.

Reagan, J. (1987). Classifying adopters and nonadopters of four technologies using Political activity, media use and demographic variables, *Telematics and Infomatics 4* (1), 3-16.

Reinard, J. (1998). *Introduction to communication research (2nd ed.)*. Boston, MA: McGraw Hill.

Robertson, R. (1970). *The sociological interpretation of religion*. Oxford: Blackwell.

Rogers, E. M. (2003). *Diffusion of innovations (5th ed.)*. New York: Free Press.

Santoro, L. (1997). Beat goes on, along with the news, as Africa's airwaves open up. *Christian Science Monitor, 89* (155), 7.

Schmitz, J. & Fulk, J. (1991). Organizational colleagues, media richness, and electronic mail: A test of the social influence model of technology use. *Communication Research 18* (4), 487-523.

Singhal, A., & Rogers, E. (2003). *Combating AIDS: Communication strategies in action*. New Delhi: Sage Publications.

Skreslet, S. H. (2007). Thinking missiologically about the history of mission. *International Bulletin of Missionary Research, 31* (2), 59-65.

Sparks, G. G. (2006). *Media effects research: A basic overview*. Belmont, CA: Thomson/Wadsworth.

Spitulnik, D. (2000). Documenting radio culture as lived experience: Reception studies & the mobile machine in Zambia. In R. Fardon & G. Furniss (Eds.), *African Broadcast Cultures: Radio in transition* (pp. 144-163). Oxford: James Currey.

Stake, R. E. (1995). *The art of case study research*. Thousand Oaks, CA: Sage.

Steel, A. (1996). *Loud let it ring: Adventist World Radio: Twenty-five years of miracles*. Boise, ID: Pacific Press publishing association.

Stoneman, T. H. B. (2006). *Capturing believers: American international radio, religion,and reception, 1931-1970*. Available from ProQuest Works and Theses database. (UMI No. 3212303).

Stoneman, T. H. B. (2007). Preparing the soil for global revival: Station HCJB's Radio Circle, 1949-59. *Church History, 76* (1), 114-155.

Straus, S. (2007). What is the relationship between hate radio and violence?

Rethinking Rwanda's "Radio Machete", *Politics Society, 35*, (4), 609-637.

Strengholt, J. M. (2008). *Gospel in the air: 50 years of Christian witness through radio in the Arab world.* The Netherlands: Boekencentrum Publishing House.

Topan, F. (1973). *Aliyeonja Pepo.* Dar es Salaam: Tanzania Publishing House. Trans. By M. Mkambo (1980) in English as A taste of heaven. Dar es Salaam: Tanzania Publishing House.

Tosh, J. (2000). *The pursuit of history (3rd ed.).* Essex, England: Pearson Education Limited.

Turner, P. R. (1979). Religious conversion and community development. *Journal for the Scientific Study of Religion, 18,* 252-60.

Vahakangas, M. (2008). Ghambageu encounters Jesus in Sonjo mythology: Syncretism as African rational action. *Journal of the American Academy of Religion, 76,* (1), 111-137.

Vaughan, P.W., & Rogers, E. M. (2000). A staged model of communication effects: Evidence from an entertainment-education radio soap opera in Tanzania. *Journal of Health Communication, 5,* 203-227.

Vernon, D. L. (2009). Assessing media effects and social change. Unpublished manuscript. Howard University, Washington, DC.

Wimmer, R. D., & Dominick, J. R. (2006). *Mass media research: An introduction* (8th ed.). Belmont, CA: Thomson Wadsworth.

Wright, C. R. (1960). Functional analysis and mass communication. *Public Opinion Quarterly*, 24, 606-20.

Wright, M. (1971). *German missions in Tanganyika, 1891-1941*. Oxford.

Tertiary Sources

Awde, N. (2000). *Swahili Practical Dictionary: Swahili-English, English-Swahili*. NY: Hippocrene Books, Inc.

Backmer, S. (2007). Adventist World Radio: Short "waves" net tall results. *Adventist World*, 16.

Berry, L. (2003). Tanzania: Population and resources. In K. Murison (Ed.), *Africa south of the Sahara 2003 (32nd ed.)*. London and New York: Europa Publications.

Cash, R. W. (1995). *United in Christ: 133rd annual statistical report 1995*. Complied by Office of Archives and Statistics. Silver Spring, MD: General Conference of Seventh-day Adventists.

Cash, R. W. (1996). *United in Christ: 134th annual statistical report 1995*. Complied by Office of Archives and Statistics. Silver Spring, MD: General Conference of Seventh-day Adventists.

Christian History Institute (2007). January 2, 1921: KDKA made religious waves. Retrieved March 10, 2008, from http://chi.gospelcom.net/DAILYF/2001/01/daily-01-01-2001.shtml.

Central Intelligence Agency (2010). *The world fact book*. Retrieved February 16, 2010 from https://www.cia.gov/library/publications/the-world-factbook/.

Cross, F. L. & Livingstone, E. A. (1997). *The Oxford dictionary of the Christian Church*. London: Oxford University Press.

ELWA Ministries. Retrieved March 10, 2008 from www.elwaministries.org.

Eliade, M. (Ed.). (1987). *The encyclopedia of religion, 5,* p. 190-191. New York: Macmillan Publishing.

General Conference Ministerial Department (1992). *Seventh-day Adventist Ministers Manual*. Hagerstown, MD: Review and herald Publishing Association.

Jones, K. (1999). *137th annual statistical report 1999*. Office of Archives and Statistics. Silver Spring, MD: General Conference of Seventh-day Adventists.

Jones, K. (2000). *138th annual statistical report 2000*. Office of Archives and

Statistics. Silver Spring, MD: General Conference of Seventh-day Adventists.

Jones, K. (2001). *139th annual statistical report 2001*. Office of Archives and Statistics. Silver Spring, MD: General Conference of Seventh-day Adventists.

Jones, K. (2002). *140th annual statistical report 2002*. Office of Archives and Statistics. Silver Spring, MD: General Conference of Seventh-day Adventists.

Jones, K. (2003). *141st annual statistical report 2003*. Office of Archives and Statistics. Silver Spring, MD: General Conference of Seventh-day Adventists.

Jones, K. (2004). *142nd annual statistical report 2004*. Office of Archives and Statistics. Silver Spring, MD: General Conference of Seventh-day Adventists.

Jones, K. & Proctor, C. (2005). *143rd annual statistical report 2005*. Office of Archives and Statistics. Silver Spring, MD: General Conference of Seventh-day Adventists.

Jones, K. & Proctor, C. (2006). *144th annual statistical report 2006*. Office of Archives and Statistics. Silver Spring, MD: General Conference of Seventh-day Adventists.

Jones, K. & Proctor, C. (2007). *145th annual statistical report 2007.* Office of Archives and Statistics. Silver Spring, MD: General Conference of Seventh-day Adventists.

Jones, K. & Proctor, C. (2008). *146th annual statistical report 2008.* Office of Archives and Statistics. Silver Spring, MD: General Conference of Seventh-day Adventists.

Jones, K. & Proctor, C. (2009). *147th annual statistical report 2009.* Office of Archives and Statistics. Silver Spring, MD: General Conference of Seventh-day Adventists.

Jones, K. & Proctor, C. (2010). *148th annual statistical report 2010.* Office of Archives and Statistics. Silver Spring, MD: General Conference of Seventh-day Adventists.

Murison, K. (Ed.). (2003). *Africa south of the Sahara 2003 (32nd ed.).* London and New York: Europa Publications.

Neufeld, D. F. (Ed.). (1996). *Seventh-day Adventist Encyclopedia (2nd ed.).* Hagerstown, MD: Review and Herald Publishing Association.

Neufeldt, V. (Ed.). (1997). *Webster's new world college dictionary (3rd ed.).* USA: Macmillan.

Pew Research Center (2010). *Tolerance and tension: Islam and Christianity in*

Sub-Saharan Africa. Washington DC: Pew Forum on Religion & Public Life.

Scragg, W. & Steele, A. (1996). *The AWR story book*. Maryland: Review and Herald Publishing Association.

Taasisi ya Uchunguzi wa Kiswahili (TUKI). (2001). *Kamusi ya Kiswahili-Kiingereza. Swahili-English Dictionary*. Dar es Salaam: TUKI.

Tanzania: Regions and districts (2011). Retrieved March 20, 2011 from http://en.wikipedia.org/wiki/Tanzania.

The Secretariat (1990). *Seventh-day Adventist Church Manual*. Silver Spring, MD: General Conference of Seventh-day Adventist.

Secretary's Statistical Report-Quarterly (2010, March). *2009 Fourth quarter secretary's statistical report-world summary*. MD: General Conference Office of Archive and Statistics.

Seventh-day Adventist Yearbook (2002). Hagerstown, MD: Review and Herald Publishing Association.

Seventh-day Adventist Yearbook (2008). Hagerstown, MD: Review and Herald Publishing Association.

Seventh-day Adventist Yearbook (2009). Hagerstown, MD: Review and Herald Publishing Association.

Seventh-day Adventist Yearbook (2010). Hagerstown, MD: Review and Herald Publishing Association.

Seventh-day Adventist Yearbook (2011). Hagerstown, MD: Review and Herald Publishing Association. Available online at http://www.adventistyearbook.org/default.aspx

Shillington, K. (Ed.). (2005). *Encyclopedia of African history, 3.* P-Z Index. NY: Fitzroy Dearborn.

Ugandaweb: Gateway to Uganda (2005). Uganda web communication section. Retrieved May 6, 2009 from http://www.ugandaweb.co.ug/communication/page.php?name=Broadcasting &loc=communication.

Van Buren, L. (2003). Tanzania: Economy. In K. Murison (Ed.), *Africa south of the Sahara 2003 (32nd ed.).* London and New York: Europa Publications.

The World Bank (2011). Tanzania. Retrieved March 7, 2011 from http://go.worldbank.org/A907QAVDA0.

Yost, F. D. (1983). 1000 days of reaping: *121st annual statistical report 1983.* Office of Archives and Statistics. Washington DC: General Conference of Seventh-day Adventists.

Yost, F. D. (1984). 1000 days of reaping: *122nd annual statistical report 1984.*

Office of Archives and Statistics. Washington DC: General Conference of Seventh-day Adventists.

Yost, F. D. (1986). *1000 days of reaping: 124th annual statistical report 1986.* Office of Archives and Statistics. Washington DC: General Conference of Seventh-day Adventists.

Yost, F. D. (1987). *Harvest 90: 125th annual statistical report 1987.* Office of Archives and Statistics. Washington DC: General Conference of Seventh-day Adventists.

Yost, F. D. (1988). *Harvest 90: 126th annual statistical report 1988.* Office of Archives and Statistics. Silver Spring, MD: General Conference of Seventh-day Adventists.

Yost, F. D. (1989). *Harvest 90: 127th annual statistical report 1989.* Office of Archives and Statistics. Silver Spring, MD: General Conference of Seventh-day Adventists.

Yost, F. D. (1990). *128th annual statistical report 1990.* Office of Archives and Statistics. Silver Spring, MD: General Conference of Seventh-day Adventists.

Yost, F. D. (1991). *129th annual statistical report 1991.* Office of Archives and Statistics. Silver Spring, MD: General Conference of Seventh-day Adventists.

Yost, F. D. (1992). *130th annual statistical report 1992.* Office of Archives and
    Statistics. Silver Spring, MD: General Conference of Seventh-day
    Adventists.

Yost, F. D. (1993). *131st annual statistical report 1993.* Office of Archives and
    Statistics. Silver Spring, MD: General Conference of Seventh-day
    Adventists.

Yost, F. D. (1994). *132nd annual statistical report 1994.* Office of Archives and
    Statistics. Silver Spring, MD: General Conference of Seventh-day
    Adventists.

Ytreberg, S. (1997). *135th annual statistical report 1997.* Office of Archives and
    Statistics. Silver Spring, MD: General Conference of Seventh-day
    Adventists.

Ytreberg, S. (1998). *136th annual statistical report 1998.* Office of Archives and
    Statistics. Silver Spring, MD: General Conference of Seventh-day
    Adventists.